Weddings

IDEAS & INSPIRATIONS FOR CELEBRATING IN STYLE

COUNTRY LIVING

Weddings

IDEAS & INSPIRATIONS FOR CELEBRATING IN STYLE

MARIE PROELLER HUESTON

HEARST BOOKS
A division of Sterling Publishing Co., Inc.

New York / London
www.sterlingpublishing.com

Contents

Foreword

There's something about a wedding that brings out the romantic in all of us. Country weddings in particular seem to delight the senses like no others. Over the years, we've featured a number of magical weddings on the pages of *Country Living*. And just as no two country homes we've shown have ever been alike, no two country weddings were quite the same. There was a lobster picnic on a Pennsylvania farm, dinner and dancing under the stars at an Oregon vineyard, a garden party at a gracious New Jersey home, and an elegant luncheon in a historic house overlooking the Hudson River. Creative ideas and personal details made each celebration unique.

Through evocative photographs and practical advice, *Weddings* will show you how to plan and personalize your own special day. If you've always imagined getting married in your parents' garden or holding your reception in an old barn but didn't know how to make it happen, we'll lead you through the process, start to finish. From picking the perfect location to choosing parting gifts that will enchant your guests and forever remind them of you, you'll find ideas and inspiration here to design the wedding of your dreams.

—The Editors of *Country Living*

Introduction

Vows exchanged beneath a canopy of blue sky, a bride and groom riding in a horse-drawn carriage, a bouquet of elegant roses interspersed with humble wildflowers, a serving table fashioned from wooden planks set atop hay bales—these are just a few of the memorable vignettes that a country wedding might include. Whether held in a sprawling vineyard, an intimate backyard, or even an urban loft transformed for the occasion, the country wedding affords couples countless opportunities to create one-of-a-kind celebrations.

But what is it that makes a wedding "country"? In years past, the term was used to refer specifically to rural celebrations, often held outdoors and with a refreshingly casual flair. These days, country weddings have little to do with a zip code or a singular design sensibility. Rather, they're all about a state of mind. Country weddings, no matter where they are held, capture the spirit of country style itself and all that it represents: home, family, tradition, comfort, and the bounty of nature.

Country weddings are popular today for a number of reasons. Part of the allure stems from the wide range of settings that are available (a beach, a barn, a botanical garden, a mountaintop). Add to this our nation's growing interest in nature-based and environmentally friendly pursuits, and the appeal becomes all the more evident. Perhaps the greatest recommendation of all is the freedom couples are afforded to chart their own path when it comes to the overall look of their day. For when putting together a country wedding, you are allowed—even encouraged—to experiment.

Weddings celebrates this sense of freedom while acknowledging that such broad creative license can sometimes be daunting. With so many locations and design possibilities to choose from, how can you determine which is the best for you? Is the beach ceremony you've always imagined a realistic option for the guests in your party? How can you locate a vineyard for your nuptials if you don't live in a wine-growing region? How can you designate a ceremony spot in the middle of an open field or bring the outdoors in to beautify an urban event? The answers to these and many more questions can be found in the pages ahead.

OPPOSITE: *Mixing traditional wedding flowers with more humble varieties is a hallmark of country style. Rich colors and unexpected additions characterize this bridal bouquet, a combination of freesia, dill, elderberries, and roses.* PAGE 6: *A carefree country wedding was this bride's dream ever since she was a little girl; her dream came true one summer day at a vineyard in Sublimity, Oregon.*

one is best suited to your needs is entirely a matter of taste.

In "Designing Your Day," we address the myriad ways you can put your own personal stamp on your wedding. You'll find hints on the details you'd expect, like invitations, flowers, and table settings, as well as a few tips on subjects you might not have considered before: incorporating your collections into your celebration, carving out cozy nooks for small groups of guests to catch up with one another, and finding fun ways to keep children entertained. A sidebar on page 62 is devoted to "do-it-yourself" ideas is sure to pique the interest of crafters.

We begin with "Choosing a Location," a rundown of the most frequently used places to hold a country wedding. In-depth descriptions of each venue will help you understand both the decorative possibilities and the work requirements. Some locations, like a farm, offer breathtaking country scenery but require a bit more legwork on your part to prepare for a formal affair. Other spots, like a country inn or a historic house, boast lovely (if less rustic) grounds and a staff of people to help you plan your day. Which

Our final chapter is "A Wedding Primer," filled with practical information on hiring a wedding planner, finding a florist, choosing a photographer, even arranging for proper lighting on your big day. In short, the primer is your tutorial to re-create the ideas pictured throughout this book. Whether you decide to reinterpret just a few of the notions you find here or to reimagine an entire celebration using your own palette and personal details, let *Weddings* be your guide.

ABOVE LEFT: *Creating cozy sitting areas encourages guests to meander through the property and sit awhile. On this New Hampshire farm, floral arrangements were even placed on the pond's dock beside two inviting Adirondack chairs.* OPPOSITE: *A farm in New Jersey is the picturesque setting for this country bride's dream day. An afternoon mist lends an air of mystery to the lush surroundings and does nothing to dampen the bride's spirits. Because the bride wanted an outdoor wedding come rain or shine, the reception was planned for a dry barn transformed for the occasion.*

1

Choosing a Location

The first—and arguably the most important—decision that all betrothed couples will face is where to celebrate their wedding. The choice of location can affect all other aspects of the day, from the size and budget of the event to the food, music, and dress. The dramatic backdrop of a horse ranch, for instance, could comfortably accommodate a large, lavish party with a western barbecue menu, a square-dance caller in lieu of a deejay, and cowboy boots for all, including the bride and her attendants. A small historic house, on the other hand, might be the better venue for an intimate affair with a lighter menu, a string quartet, and perhaps an antique wedding gown.

Where to Wed?

To find the perfect place for you, begin by picturing your ideal wedding day. Where do you see yourself exchanging vows or dancing your first dance as a married couple? A beach at sunset? A mountaintop? A grand ballroom filled with flowers? Once you have a clear picture of your dream wedding in your head, the next step is to analyze the particulars of your wedding plan, including the budget, the guest list, and the amount of physical work that will be involved to prepare the venue. The "Location Checklist" on page 45 outlines the major questions to consider. If no single place comes to mind, don't despair: The following pages discuss the pros and cons of a number of popular options to help you find the one that's right for you.

Farm

A symbol of our nation's enduring connection to the land, a farm may well be the quintessential country wedding location. The backdrop is hard to beat: verdant fields and rolling hills punctuated by strong architectural elements like steel-gray silos and big red barns. Add to this vision a hand-hewn wood fence (perfect for garlands) or a horse contentedly grazing in a meadow, and it's no wonder so many couples dream of being wed in such a

place. Farm weddings tend to be somewhat relaxed in style, but the size and scale of the setting mean there is more than enough room to interpret your day exactly as you see it: It could be black tie, country casual, or comfortably in between.

There are seasonal considerations when planning a farm wedding. Since most events are held at least partially outdoors, warmer months are chosen most frequently. An apple orchard in bloom could form a breathtaking canopy for a springtime ceremony, while summer's bounty of fruits and vegetables could be incorporated into the dinner menu or be given to guests as parting gifts. Fall weddings might feature warm mulled cider and a hayride for children. Although less common, winter farm weddings are not unheard of. As long as indoor space is sufficient, an event at this frosty time of year can actually be quite romantic: Imagine a warm barn filled with

Green TIP

If holding your wedding on an organic farm, ask your caterer if the farm's produce or dairy products can be incorporated into the menu.

LEFT: *The first two floors of the bride's family's six-story barn were taken over for the reception. Because the cupola-topped, post-and-beam building was recently erected by a local New Hampshire carpenter, the family did not need to assess its structural integrity beforehand, as you would need to do if planning to hold a reception in a century-old barn.* BELOW: *Old farm tables can be used in myriad ways at an outdoor wedding. Placed around the property, they can serve any number of purposes: supporting the guest book, providing a spot for cocktail service, displaying the wedding cake, or just acting as a gathering place for small groups of family and friends. This wonderfully weathered table is dressed in a blue-and-white toile tablecloth—the signature colors of the wedding.*

fragrant flowers and twinkling lights set against a stark, snowy landscape.

When scouting a farm for your wedding day, look for picturesque spots for the ceremony and practical spots for the reception. A grove of trees, some level ground in front of a pretty pond, or a meadow dotted around the edges with Queen Anne's lace would all work well for a ceremony. Receptions can be held in the open air, beneath a tent, or inside a barn. Whether under a tent or under the stars, outdoor reception sites need to be as flat as possible to accommodate tables and a dance floor. Barns should be structurally sound, broom clean, and free of any evidence of animal inhabitants by the day of the wedding. And while the nearby sound of a whinnying horse can add to the authentic feeling of a farm wedding, it's best to maintain a comfortable distance between farm animals and the events of the day.

Farm weddings are a romantic ideal for many couples, but they take careful planning and, oftentimes, significant elbow grease to pull together. Cleaning out a barn can be a time-consuming project, but it's a task someone else can do for you if your budget allows. A tent is a common solution, in cases where a large clean barn is not available for the reception. Parking, portable restrooms, electricity for a band or for lighting a barn, and a contingency plan for inclement weather are some of the other issues that might need to be addressed.

So where do couples find the perfect farm for a wedding? Many have a personal connection to the place, like a family farm where the bride or groom grew up or the farm of a close friend or relative. This can be an advantage when it comes to planning, as you might feel greater freedom to explore all corners of the farm and could even use the farmhouse as a home base. If no friend or family member lives on a farm, however, take heart: There are other options. Begin by asking friends, work colleagues, and shopkeepers if they know of farms in the area that have hosted weddings. Wedding professionals in your area (planners, caterers, florists) may also know of a spot. Farms that welcome the public—ones that have pick-your-own produce, for example—are likely to be more open to the idea than others. If you and your fiancé had a memorable date picking apples at a local farm, why not approach the owner?

𝐵ottom line: **A farm is the right location for you if you want a beautiful, rustic backdrop for your wedding and are comfortable with the extra work that may be required to get the space ready for a formal event.**

OPPOSITE: *Take advantage of striking architectural elements on a farm to create unforgettable pictures, like the loft door at the top of this barn. If you're able, tour your wedding location with your photographer before the big day so together you can spot memorable settings ahead of time.*

ABOVE: *The path leading to the ceremony is lined with dowels embellished with streamers and sap buckets filled with loose arrangements of summer blooms: hydrangea, zinnias, and black-eyed Susans.* RIGHT: *A wagon wheel dressed with roses and ribbons marks the site of a wedding ceremony beneath two tall oaks. Above the wheel, a garland of sunflowers and greenery stretches between the two trunks.* OPPOSITE: *The bride and her father make their way down a path beneath a canopy of old oaks. Guests lined the path to watch the processional then follow behind to witness the ceremony. The father of the bride heeded his daughter's request to ditch the stuffy suit. "Jeans and black suspenders—that's the Daddy I know," she explains.*

Barn Basics

Almost any barn can be used for a wedding as long as it can comfortably accommodate your guests, is structurally sound, and was not recently used to house animals. Barns come in all shapes and sizes. Some farm owners have converted their barns (indeed, sometimes their entire farm) into venues used exclusively for weddings and other events by renovating the structure and adding restrooms, handicapped access, and additional amenities to accommodate vendors and large groups of people. Barns that haven't been renovated may be less polished but still offer a weathered, rustic appeal. Here are basic tips to help you choose the right barn and prepare it for your big day.

WHICH BARN IS BEST? The size of your guest list will be an important factor in finding the right barn, along with how you plan to use the space. Will you set up dinner tables in the barn or simply use it for dancing, after dinner has been served outdoors or in a tent? If you're serving dinner in the barn, is there space for the caterer to set up a kitchen and, if not, is there space next door for the caterer with a clear pathway for the wait staff to travel between the two locations? Are there restrooms nearby, and is the barn easily accessible for handicapped guests or those with limited mobility?

DETERMINE STRUCTURAL INTEGRITY. If you have any doubts as to the condition of your barn, especially an older barn, hire a structural engineer to survey the site. You can find someone through companies that conduct home inspections.

A CLEAN SWEEP. Barns are rustic by nature, so you don't need to make the interior spotless. Sweep the floor well, remove any cobwebs from beams and rafters, and wash the windows.

CONSIDER LIGHTING. If a barn is not already wired, talk to an electrician about lighting options such as wiring the building or running a generator to power spotlights for a band and strings of lights to decorate the rafters.

FIRE SAFETY. Install several fire extinguishers throughout the space in case of emergencies. Be sure tables are positioned far enough apart to create clear paths in the event that a quick exit from the barn is necessary.

OPPOSITE: *Paper lanterns, twinkling white lights, and boughs of white pine bring a fairy-tale quality to a rustic barn. The soaring ceilings and the graphic lines of the rafters are reminiscent of a grand cathedral.*

ᴇ◦◦ Vineyard ◦◦ᴈ

Like farms, vineyards appeal to couples who dream of an outdoor wedding, surrounded by nature and the fruits of the land. Vineyards tend to have a more orderly feeling about them than farms, a likely result of the rows upon rows of grapevines that crisscross the land. In some ways, the process of planning a vineyard wedding can be more orderly as well. Since many vineyards host weddings on a regular basis, the owners may already work with local caterers, bakers, florists, and tent rental companies, thereby taking much of the guesswork out of the process. (They may even have a wedding planner on staff.) Vineyards are especially ideal for couples with a passion for food and wine, offering them the opportunity to work with the vintner to create special food and wine pairings from the cocktail hour through the dessert course.

The peak wedding season for vineyards is late summer into fall, when the vines are heavy with grapes and lush green leaves. Late-fall foliage can make a spectacular backdrop for a vineyard wedding, but the air can be chilly, especially in the evening, so it may not be the best time of year if you wish to hold the ceremony and reception outdoors. Winter and spring are not the most desirable times for a vineyard wedding;

Green TIP

Having your ceremony and reception in the same location eliminates the transportation needed to ferry guests between two spots.

but if you find beauty in the off-season landscape, it may be a good way to reduce costs for your dream day if the vineyard's rental fees are lower than at other times of the year.

If the vineyard has hosted weddings before, inquire where other couples have held their ceremonies and receptions. Knowing where the prettiest spots are in advance—a century-old oak tree, a gazebo, or a hilltop vista, for instance—can save you the time of scouting for yourself. Many vineyard receptions are held outdoors (look for flat ground for open-air tables or a tent), but an indoor reception might also be possible. Depending on the size of your guest list, some vineyards have large enclosed spaces or tasting rooms that can elegantly accommodate dinner and dancing. Whether outdoors or in, be sure that the seating arrangement provides you and your guests a full view of the beautiful surroundings.

Some vineyards have a wedding planner on staff; if so, consider taking advantage of her or his assistance when planning your day. As with

OPPOSITE: *A hillside view reveals the beauty of Oregon's Willamette Valley. Dining tables, a dance floor, and a stage strung with paper lanterns are arranged on the flat lawn surrounding the vineyard's main building.*

Guests wave sparklers to greet the bride and groom at this vineyard wedding. A passion for Latin foods and music influenced the design choices for the celebration, including the vibrant colors of the brides- maid dresses and paper lanterns as well as the band playing lively Cuban music.

other outdoor venues, weather can be an issue at a vineyard. Ask about alternative plans in the event of inclement weather: Is there enough indoor space to accommodate your guests if it should rain? Another consideration is that some vineyards are open to the public on weekends for tours and wine tastings. You'll want to know ahead of time if this will be the case on your wedding day. If you are unable to have the grounds entirely to yourself, ask how your event will be demarcated to prevent other people from popping in on the ceremony and reception.

Vineyards are found in areas of the country that have the proper growing conditions for grapes: California, Oregon, Washington, and Upstate New York are the major regions in the United States. If you live within driving distance of these areas, conduct an Internet search of vineyards in the region and take a weekend road trip to visit them. Tour the grounds, speak with the staff about their wedding policies, and be sure to attend a wine tasting if you can. For couples who live far from a wine-growing region, a vineyard wedding offers the opportunity for a destination wedding: You could plan an entire weekend away for your guests to stay in a nearby country inn and enjoy local activities before and after the wedding. Travel guides and Internet searches of vineyards in a particular state are a good way to get started.

Bottom line: A vineyard is the right location for you if you want a picturesque outdoor setting and less hands-on preparation than traditional farm weddings. Vineyards are also a good choice for couples passionate about food and wine.

At Home

What more personal place could there be for a wedding than a home that holds fond memories for you or your fiancé? It may be a house you grew up in, one where you spent your summer vacations as a child, or one that you purchased together as a couple. It may even be the home of a generous friend whose offer to host your wedding adds a new chapter in the ongoing story of your friendship. In truth, any home can be used, as long as it can comfortably accommodate your guests. To allow ample room for mingling, dining, and dancing, a generously proportioned garden or a roomy interior is a must. As long as there is enough space to work with, homes in all styles and in all parts of the country can be transformed into the ideal setting.

The first question to ask is whether you plan to hold both the ceremony and the reception at home. Plenty of couples do so, while others choose to have the ceremony in a local church or town hall and then return home for the reception. If you wish to use the garden for your ceremony or reception (as many couples do), warm months are the logical choice. Imagine the beauty of a late-spring or early-summer garden fragrant with hyacinth, lilac, and roses. Late-summer events can take advantage of warm evenings for dancing under the stars. And as long as space is not an issue, cold-weather weddings can be stunning indoors in rooms aglow with candlelight.

When scouting suitable places to hold outdoor ceremonies, look for focal points in the garden that can be a backdrop for your vows. Perhaps there is a rose trellis, a gazebo, or a tall tree that can be festooned with ribbons. If planning an indoor ceremony, find interior focal points: a sunny bay window, an elegant mantel, or a grand staircase in a spacious entryway. Outdoor reception sites should be wide and flat: a large lawn, a rose garden, or the paved surface surrounding a pool. (Pools look lovely when flowers or votive candles are set afloat.) A tent is a wise choice for outdoor receptions, unless the house is nearby and has room to accommodate everyone in the event of rain. Indoor receptions generally take over the first floor of a house, with furniture in the living room and dining room replaced by tables and chairs. An advantage to indoor receptions is that you'll spend less time worrying about the possibility of rain, pesky insects, and extreme heat or chill.

Anyone who has watched Spencer Tracy trying to navigate the flurry of activity that preceded Elizabeth Taylor's at-home wedding in 1950's *Father of the Bride* (or Steve Martin and Kimberly Williams in the 1991 remake) knows that weddings at home take a great deal of planning. You may need to touch up paint and floors indoors or spruce up the garden by trimming hedges, repaving paths, and installing outdoor lighting. In some cases, you may even want to hire a landscaper to redesign the grounds or simply plant more flowers. If you plan to welcome your guests indoors, you'll probably need to remove some or all of the furniture to allow for better traffic flow and to accommodate tables and chairs for dining. Many couples staging at-home weddings rent one or two portable restrooms and situate them outside and away from the main ceremony and reception sites. Parking can also be an issue. If space is limited, ask neighbors if they would be willing to lend their driveways for the day (inviting them to the wedding would be a gracious thank-you), or arrange for a van or shuttle bus to and from a local parking garage.

Quite often, the house or garden of the bride's or groom's parents is the site of an at-home wedding. Other hosts might be members of your extended family such as grandparents, godparents, uncles, and aunts. If you feel that the home of relatives or friends would be the perfect spot for your wedding, approach them with the knowledge that preparing for a wedding is a big undertaking: Don't hold it against them if they'd prefer to be guests at your wedding rather than the hosts. Be considerate of your hosts by sharing with them your vision of the day. Consult with them when making arrangements or anticipating deliveries. Holding a wedding at your own home lessens the need to coordinate with others and has an added benefit for couples who love spontaneity: You can invite guests for a housewarming, a holiday gathering, or a New Year's party and then surprise them with a wedding!

Bottom line: At home is the right location for you if you want a strong personal connection to the setting, have access to a home or garden that can accommodate your party, and are comfortable with the work it will take to prepare the space for your big day.

OPPOSITE: *Guests await the bride and groom at a waterside setting. When scouting an outdoor locale for the best place to hold your ceremony, look for a focal point, like this towering tree.*

OPPOSITE: *Carve out secluded spots where small groups of guests can gather. This magical setting is created with a simple tent, garden benches softened with plush pillows, potted lilacs, and a meandering path of votive candles.* LEFT: *A wide, flat lawn is essential for anyone wishing to raise a tent for an outdoor wedding. For this happy couple, the backyard of the bride's parents' New Jersey home provided just such a setting. Their summer nuptials featured a ceremony in the garden followed by dining and dancing under a spacious white tent.* BELOW: *An elegant entrance can set the tone for a wedding. After arriving in a horse-drawn carriage, this country bride passes through a grape arbor and into the garden of her uncle's Connecticut home, where her betrothed awaits.*

Beach

The relaxed atmosphere and natural beauty of the beach emanate classic country style, making it an unforgettable spot for a wedding. Couples who choose a beach wedding often have a personal connection to the sea: They may live in a beach community or they may have spent their childhood summers in a picturesque coastal town. Others have simply fallen under the spell of this romantic location and can't imagine exchanging vows anywhere else. Owing to the wind-swept nature of this setting, beach weddings almost always exhibit a casual, laid-back style. Couples dreaming of a more formal affair can still make it happen here, especially if a ceremony on the beach is followed by a reception at a local hotel, restaurant, or club.

Summertime is the most popular choice for beach weddings. Anyone marrying in cooler months may find an indoor setting with an ocean view a suitable alternative. Make the day a celebration of the surroundings: Use seashells and beach colors in your decorating scheme, tuck beach roses and tall grasses into your floral arrangements, and incorporate fresh seafood into your menu. You might even consider a traditional clambake or lobster dinner. The beach also offers endless inspiration for playful details: Flower girls can carry beach pails filled with rose petals, for example, while a guest book can be positioned on a small wooden table beneath a colorful beach umbrella. (Weight the book down with pretty beach stones if ocean breezes are strong.)

Ceremonies on the beach usually have the bride and groom standing closest to the water, with guests looking out toward the horizon. A couple might also stand in the center of their guests, who are gathered in a circle around them. You'll want to decide if your guests will stand, as many do at beach locales, or sit during the ceremony. If seating will be necessary, opt for wooden benches or beach chairs that won't sink into the sand as much as traditional tapered-leg chairs. If the area includes both ocean and bayside beaches, note that shorelines near a bay tend to be quieter and less windy than those at the ocean. If you choose to have your ceremony on an ocean beach, consider setting up a microphone so that your guests will be able to hear you and your officiant clearly.

Many couples choose to follow a beach ceremony with a reception at a separate place nearby, be it a hotel, a beach club, or a private home. This is certainly the simpler road to take, since catering a large meal in a sandy setting can be challenging—but certainly not impossible.

OPPOSITE: *Slipcovered chairs await guests at this seaside ceremony, proving that beach weddings can be formal in character. White Aztec calla lilies adorn the bamboo huppa. A mat made from coconut fiber and biodegradable resin lines the aisle, making it easier for the wedding party and guests to walk across the sand.*

Planning an indoor reception also means less worrying about the chance of inclement or windy beach weather. That said, a casual clambake or other reception right on the beach can be wonderful. Check beach regulations for the town or village where the beach is located; there may be restrictions about food, glassware, and alcohol on the beach. It's also imperative to check the schedule of tides and to plan your day accordingly. Be sure to inform guests ahead of time about the beach setting so they may dress appropriately. Many brides choose ankle-length dresses to keep hems out of the sand.

The amount of hands-on preparation needed to transform your dream of a beach wedding into a reality will depend a lot on your vision for the day. One scenario might have guests gathering on the beach, standing during the ceremony, and walking or driving to a reception at a nearby restaurant, hotel, or home. A more elaborate scheme might involve setting up a true altar, aisle, and seating on the beach followed by a sit-down dinner on the sand with live music and perhaps a bonfire after dark. Whether you'll simply exchange vows on the beach or host the entire event there, having an alternative plan in the event of rain is a must.

If you have friends or family members with a home near or on the beach, they are the first people to speak to about bringing your dream wedding to life. If, on the other hand, you've fallen in love with a beach or a coastal town but don't have a personal connection to the area, contact the local chamber of commerce to find out more about hosting an event on one of the town's beaches. Caterers in the area may have handled beach weddings before, so they may be able to tell you which locations are best suited to a wedding ceremony or reception. Some seaside hotels offer wedding packages, and you might even decide on a destination wedding, with a smaller group of guests spending a whole weekend away and the hotel making most of the arrangements.

Bottom line: **A beach is the right location for you if you feel a strong connection to the seashore, if you envision a wedding day that is casual in spirit, and if you welcome the challenge of creating a wedding atmosphere in a raw yet beautiful setting.**

Botanical Garden

A bustling city may lie just beyond the walls of a botanical garden, but upon its grounds you feel far away from it all. Paths wind through alleys of tall oaks and groves of fragrant lilacs, thousands of spring bulbs bloom simultaneously, lily pads float atop tranquil turtle ponds. Beyond the natural beauty of the setting, most botanical

FAR LEFT: *Having fallen in love with the lush grounds and breathtaking view of the Hudson River from Wave Hill, a historic house and garden in Riverdale, New York, one couple chose to wait more than a year to hold their wedding there, when the glory of the spring garden would be at its peak.* NEAR LEFT: *Built in 1843, the English cottage–style mansion of Wave Hill continues to capture the imaginations of the betrothed couples who choose to hold their weddings there each year.*

gardens are well equipped to host weddings. At many gardens across the country, gleaming glass conservatories and wide lawns are available for receptions, and charming spots to exchange vows can be found throughout the grounds.

While botanical gardens with ample indoor space are suitable for weddings year-round (off-season rental rates are usually lower, too), the most popular time of year by far is late spring through the end of summer, when the blooming annuals and perennials really put on a show. Some couples plan their wedding to coincide with peak seasons, such as cherry blossom time in early spring or the midsummer rose garden. If you dream of a backdrop of colorful blossoms

for your big day, ask if it's possible to have your wedding on the grounds, under trees in bloom or among landscaped flower beds. Other times of year offer equally stunning vignettes: Fall foliage can be breathtaking, for instance, especially if you incorporate the colors of the season into your decorating scheme. And even winter's frost cannot dim the glow of a conservatory trimmed with twinkling lights.

Rules vary from one botanical garden to the next regarding where a wedding ceremony or reception may be held. Some have designated spots already in place and little flexibility. Others allow couples to hold the ceremony—and occasionally the reception—on the grounds in the spot of their choosing. If you are able to choose, set aside an afternoon to roam the grounds and search for pretty settings. You might also do as some couples do and have your ceremony in a local church or town hall followed by a reception at the garden. If the weather is warm and clear, consider holding at least part of the reception outdoors, even if dining and dancing will take place inside a conservatory or under a tent. Serving appetizers and cocktails around a beautiful fountain or beneath a pagoda in an Asian garden can be a lovely segue from ceremony to reception.

Because so many botanical gardens host weddings, it is often the case that much of the preparation has already been done for you, especially if there is a conservatory or a lawn designated for tents. Parking and restrooms, for example, are usually sufficient for a reasonably large party. If a wedding planner is on staff, ask if there is a list of caterers, florists, and musicians who have done weddings there before. Sometimes a botanical garden has exclusive contracts with caterers and other service providers. If this is the case, schedule a tasting with the caterers to sample their menu. You also want to find out if the garden will remain open to the public at the

time of your wedding. Many gardens schedule weddings only after they have closed to the public, and this is wise: Strolling visitors might interrupt your service or cause confusion at the reception.

Most major metropolitan areas have at least one botanical garden, and many smaller towns have one as well. Conduct a statewide Internet search or call your local chamber of commerce if you do not know of any gardens near you. If there are more than one within easy driving distance, visit each and tour the grounds. Some gardens are large and grand with multiple conservatories and acres to explore; others are smaller and more intimate. Choose the one that best conveys the style of wedding you want to create. Final words of advice: Avoid gardens that have no usable indoor space or room for a tent. Having access to a covered area in case of inclement weather is a must for any outdoor affair.

𝓑ottom line: **A botanical garden is the right location for you if you want to be surrounded by nature—especially blooming plants and trees—and if you like the idea that the setting has hosted many weddings before yours and probably has a routine already in place. Botanical gardens are also ideal for a country-in-the-city event.**

OPPOSITE: *Intimate garden gatherings can be lovely for wedding receptions as well as bridal showers and fare-well brunches. To add a touch of glamour to this garden luncheon, an iron votive chandelier is suspended from a sufficiently strong branch overhead. Decorative details include a garland of crystals, and bud vases with blooms that complement the palette of the place settings. On the table, pillar candles are set in large glass jars partially filled with water and dotted with floating roses.*

OPPOSITE: *Shaded from the sun and cooled by overhead fans, tables at this farm wedding offer guests panoramic views of verdant fields and gently rolling hills.* **ABOVE:** *Tents transform bare outdoor space into a festive reception site. Styles vary so be sure to ask the tent rental company to show you all available styles. At this garden wedding, the tent's double-peaked top and wide scalloped edge complement the stately home it stands beside.*

ᔐ Hotels and Inns ᔑ

A welcoming atmosphere with a staff waiting to help you plan your perfect day—it's no wonder that charming hotels and inns are a popular choice for couples today. Although any hotel's reception hall can be stylishly transformed with flowers, linens, and decorations, quaint country inns and smaller city hotels with lovely architectural details have a certain ambience that makes them especially well suited to creating a wedding with country spirit. You might consider reserving a block of rooms for your guests (or the entire inn) and hosting a wedding weekend, with rehearsal dinner, reception, and farewell brunch all held on the property. Depending on the hotel's offerings, spa services, nature walks, a croquet match, and afternoon tea can be placed on the itinerary as well.

Hotels and inns are open year-round, so your wedding can be held in any season of your choosing. Spring and summer are the natural choices if you want to celebrate some or all of your wedding outdoors. Many properties boast landscaped grounds with flower gardens and wide lawns ideal for tents. Fall weddings, too, can be held outdoors if the weather is mild, with guests gathering indoors

for dinner and dancing. Winter weddings can be wonderfully festive at a hotel: Guests come in from the cold to find rooms filled with fresh flowers, candlelight, and the sound of laughter.

If you plan to hold both your ceremony and reception at a hotel or inn, you'll need to seek out the best spots on the property for both parts of the day. If your wedding will be held at a country inn during warm weather, consider an outdoor ceremony. Tour the grounds and look for places that catch your eye, like a rose garden, a grassy

OPPOSITE: *Dining beneath a canopy of green leaves is an experience your guests will always remember. For this alfresco reception, table settings are kept simple to blend in with the natural surroundings. Similar arrangements are best suited to areas of the country and times of the year when you can be almost certain that inclement weather will not threaten your day.* ABOVE: *At either end of a banquet table, arrangements of roses, ivy, and amaranth spill over antique silver candlesticks loaned by a friend—a memorable "something borrowed."*

Tents 101

Tents can make any setting, no matter how rustic, suitable for a formal affair. They can act as a simple shelter for dining and dancing or they can be transformed into a fairyland interior with lights, flowers, and flowing fabrics. Here, everything you need to know if you're considering using a tent at your wedding.

ENVISION YOUR PERFECT TENT STYLE. Will you have one large tent or a few of varying sizes—a smaller tent for cocktails, perhaps, and a larger one for dinner? Would you prefer a basic white tent with open sides or something with color or decorative details?

FIND A RENTAL COMPANY YOU TRUST. Ask a wedding planner, caterer, florist, or friends for a recommendation. If you attended a wedding or other event that was held in a tent, ask the hosts what company they used.

ASK FOR A CONSULTATION. Have a representative of the tent company survey the location to advise you on the tent size you will need, the styles that are available, and the approximate cost for the day. Meet with more than one company and choose the one whose costs and overall professionalism impress you the most.

SPLURGE ON FLOORING. Rain even a day or so before the wedding can cause damp ground that could damage shoes and clothing. Flooring will also make it safer and easier for guests to walk and mingle among tables during the reception.

CHECK WITH YOUR LOCAL TOWN HALL FOR RULES AND REGULATIONS ABOUT tents . Many rental companies handle the permits that may be required, but it's wise to double-check in advance so there are no surprises as your wedding day nears.

HAVE A TENT PROFESSIONAL AT THE WEDDING. Ask that a representative from the rental company be on-site the day of the wedding to handle any problems that may arise. Even if an extra cost involved, the peace of mind is worth it.

OPPOSITE: *Choosing all white for the tent, chairs, and linens creates an ethereal atmosphere at this backyard wedding. The sides of the tent are left open to create an airy feeling and to afford guests unobstructed views of the lush garden surroundings. Laying down a dance floor is considered a must for most couples; if your budget allows, you might choose flooring for the entire length of the tent.*

lawn, a pond or fountain, or a covered porch that can be decked with flower garlands. Indoors, a bright sunroom, dining room, or ballroom can work well. To bring the outdoors in, create an archway of flowers at the end of an aisle and attach clusters of fragrant blooms to your guests' chairs. If there is an event planner on staff, ask where other couples have exchanged vows and see which places spark your imagination. Outdoor receptions can be held in the garden or under a tent, while indoor events are usually in a dining room or ballroom. Many hotels and inns are known for their creative cuisine; choosing such a property and letting the chef create a special wedding menu will be a memorable treat for your guests.

Most hotels and inns are accustomed to planning events, so there will likely be a person or staff available to help you design a one-of-a-kind celebration. Basic guest conveniences such as lodging, parking, and restrooms are taken care of, so you can focus your attention on personalizing the banquet space and as much of the property as is appropriate. For example, if you've rented an entire small country inn for a weekend, ask if your florist can adorn the public areas of the inn—an elaborate garland above the entrance, perhaps, or large arrangements in the lobby.

You may already know of a charming hotel or inn where you would like to hold your wedding. If so, don't hesitate to call and reserve a date: Hotel rooms and banquet facilities are booked far in advance. To find a location you might like to use, conduct an Internet search for inns in a particular area. Many states have hotel and country inn associations that can help you find the size and style of property that's right for you. Take a weekend drive and take a tour, eat a meal, or spend a night at any hotel you're considering. Be sure to call in advance to set up an appointment with an event planner who can explain the wedding packages and procedures. A hotel wedding is also a wonderful opportunity for a destination weekend; research hotels in an area you've always wanted to visit or one that is known for outdoor activities.

𝓑ottom line: **A hotel or an inn is the right location for you if you love the feeling of hospitality these venues offer, if you dream of a wedding weekend with your guests, and if you welcome the assistance of a staff planner to design your day.**

OPPOSITE: *Not all tents are white, so inquire at several tent rental companies until you find the style and color you envision. Sheer draped curtains in rich hues personalize this outdoor affair. Colored lights can also create dramatic effects when shining on tents or surrounding foliage.*

ꞈ Country Club ꞈ

A long driveway flanked by towering trees winds its way through beautiful landscaped grounds and leads visitors to the door of a stately building with old-world charm. This vision of how guests might arrive at a wedding is a big draw for couples who choose to hold their nuptials at a country club. Country clubs combine the beauty of nature with elegant reception halls and attentive service. Although most clubs are private, many will rent their dining rooms and banquet facilities for nonmember parties. If you (or someone you know) are a member, however, you'll be granted wider access to the grounds and can even coordinate a round of golf or spa services for your bridal party before the wedding.

Any season is suitable for a country club wedding. Late spring and early summer, when the gardens are in full bloom, are popular. In fact, all warm months are desirable in bucolic settings such as these, particularly if a club has space for outdoor events, such as a wide terrace, a lawn, or a tent area. Cold-weather weddings are held indoors and might even be easier to schedule than at the busier times of year. Late December and early January can be a lovely time to be married: Oftentimes holiday decorations like wreaths, garlands, and lights are still up,

bestowing a festive quality on the surroundings. Rates for winter weddings are usually lower as well.

If you are considering a country club, make an appointment with the wedding planner on staff and ask where ceremonies and receptions have taken place in the past. Ask about outdoor wedding options, such as a rose garden or tent. A terrace can be a lovely setting for an outdoor ceremony. You might set up a pretty archway or altar at the edge of the terrace overlooking the grounds; cocktails and music can await your guests indoors immediately following the ceremony. The planner will also help you decide the best time of day for your reception, whether you envision an afternoon luncheon or an evening bash.

At most country clubs, the event planners will assist you with every aspect of your wedding. There may be a chef on staff, and in some cases you will not be able to bring in an outside caterer. Schedule a tasting and even a meeting with the chef if you have specific ideas about your wedding menu. Ask, too, about bakers and florists—does the club arrange for both or will you be able to hire an outside source? Flowers will be key to imbuing country charm in the banquet hall, so you'll want to know early on which providers you can work with. You might take a cue from

Location Checklist

The following questions are important to consider when choosing a wedding site. When scouting locations, be sure to bring a camera and take photographs—they'll help remind you of each location you've visited.

DO YOU FEEL A PERSONAL CONNECTION TO THE PLACE? Whether it's a rugged outdoor venue or a grandparent's country retreat, a sense of connection will help the wedding reflect the taste and personality of the bride and groom.

CAN THE SITE ACCOMMODATE YOUR GUESTS COMFORTABLY? Keep in mind the size of your party—be it twenty or two hundred—and whether there will be accessibility issues for young children, disabled guests, or elderly relatives.

CAN YOU ENVISION DISTINCT AREAS FOR THE CEREMONY AND THE RECEPTION? The most picturesque spots for ceremonies often include a focal point (such as an altar or a mantelpiece indoors; perhaps a rose garden or hilltop vista outdoors). Receptions require flat open spaces for the tables, dance floor, and tent (if used).

IS THE LOCATION EASILY ACCESSIBLE? This is a consideration not only for guests but also for caterers, florists, and other hired services needed to make your dream a reality.

HOW MUCH WORK IS INVOLVED TO PREPARE THE LOCATION? Some couples embrace the hard work and advance planning that off-the-beaten-path settings like a barn or a beach generally require. Others prefer something a little less labor-intensive, such as a country club or a botanical garden.

WHAT WILL THE WEATHER BE LIKE AT THIS LOCATION? The venue may picturesque, but consider what you can't see: the climate. Spend some time researching average temperatures for that area during the month you'll be getting married, and consider contingency plans so that you'll be prepared if the temperature rises or drops. Take into account whether the site has enough space to set up a tent in the event of rain, or if it has an alternative indoor location.

WILL THE VENUE BE UNDERGOING ANY CONSTRUCTION DURING THE WEEK YOU'LL BE GETTING MARRIED? Ask the venue representative if any renovations or construction are planned for the site. You won't want construction noise competing with your ceremony and party, nor do you want the lovely surroundings spoiled by unsightly piles of debris.

the gardens at the country club. If roses or hydrangeas or irises will be in bloom at the time of your wedding, why not work those into your bouquet and table arrangements?

You may already know of a country club in your town or a nearby locale. You may even be a member. If not, the first step to finding one for your wedding will be to ask people around you, including friends, relatives, and work colleagues. Once you've found one or several clubs that sound promising, contact the event planning department and ask for an appointment to tour the grounds and reception facilities. You do not have to be a member, or even to know one, to be able to hold your wedding at most country clubs, but as we stated before, being a member will likely grant you wider access to the grounds and perhaps priority when it comes to reserving a date.

Bottom line: A country club is the right location for you if you want beautiful scenery, an elegant banquet space, and an experienced planner to help you with your wedding.

Historic House

So much of American country style is rooted in tradition and true down-home spirit. What better place, then, to host a country wedding than a location where our forefathers walked, slept, and lived their lives. Historic houses in the United States span many eras—Colonial, Federal, Victorian, and Mission, to name a few. Some are large and grand, others small and intimate. If the idea intrigues you, it's worth exploring the many options available to choose from. You might even take design cues from the age and style of a house when it comes to food, flowers, music, dress, and table settings.

The policies of each historic house will govern whether you can hold your wedding indoors or out, and that in turn may affect what time of year you have your wedding. Houses that are largely unfurnished inside, for example, are usually available for both indoor and outdoor events. Those that feature period-perfect interiors often allow only outdoor celebrations. Open-air settings for a ceremony or reception might include a flower garden, a terrace, a grove of old trees, or a lawn with the architecture of the house as a background. Indoors, look for pleasant spots such as a parlor with a marble mantel, a gracious foyer, a sunny conservatory, or an elegant ballroom. It's wise to choose a property with at least some indoor space or room for a tent so you and your guests can take cover in case of rain.

OPPOSITE: *Some aspect of the location you choose for your wedding should capture your heart, whether it's an unforgettable view, a fragrant rose garden, or a beautiful structure like this Victorian home with gingerbread trim.*

While many historic houses rent out their rooms or grounds for private parties, few have a full-time event planner on staff. This means the logistics of preparing the space for a wedding will fall largely on you or your own wedding planner. Ask whether the historic house you're considering has a list of preferred providers when it comes to catering, flowers, and music. It might be helpful to use businesses that are already familiar with the house and grounds, but if you have someone else in mind, there's no harm in asking if it's possible to bring in an outside source and if any additional fees apply.

You may already know of one or more historic houses near you. Often, a town's historical society is located in a historic house and the staff there likely has a list of other properties in the area. You can also conduct Internet searches for historic houses in a certain city or state. Call to inquire whether weddings can be held in the house or on the property, and then plan a visit. Once you've found the place that feels right to you, consider using an image of the house on your invitations and other wedding stationery. You might even research the era the house was built in and incorporate design elements into your day, such as Colonial-style bonnets for your flower girls or Victorian flourishes on your wedding program.

Bottom line: A historic house is the right location for you if you want there to be a historical aspect to your day and if you feel comfortable with all the organization it may take to coordinate the day.

Restaurant

Imagine the chef at your favorite eatery creating a wedding menu just for you. Now picture yourself enjoying the meal with your closest family and friends in the same setting where you've been on romantic dates with your fiancé. The restaurant might be the place where you had your first date, where you became engaged, or where you return again and again for special occasions. Like a vineyard wedding, a restaurant is a good choice for couples who are passionate about food and wine.

Even though restaurants are indoor spaces, seasonal considerations may still come up as you plan your wedding. If there is a pretty garden you'd love to use, you'll need to book the space in warmer months. A restaurant on a hillside above a picturesque valley may be ideal for an autumn wedding to take full advantage of the fall foliage. And cozy taverns with crackling fireplaces can be lovely for winter weddings. The time of year that you marry (even the time of day) can affect the overall cost of your wedding. A Saturday dinner in June, for example, will be more expensive than a Sunday luncheon in March, so keep this in mind when setting a date.

Depending on the size of the space and the length of your guest list (restaurants tend to work best for smaller weddings), you might choose to hold your ceremony elsewhere and then convene for a memorable meal. Larger spaces can accommodate a ceremony as well as a reception. Ask the manager or event planner what has been done in the past and imagine the room transformed for the day. In some cases, tables can be pushed aside for a ceremony, then repositioned during cocktail hour. There may be a separate area such as a garden, terrace, or sunroom where you can exchange vows and then enter the dining room as husband and wife.

One challenge of a restaurant wedding can be how to put your own stamp on a setting that already has a distinctive look. To work around this, choose a spot where the décor already reflects your taste and then speak with the staff about ways to personalize it further. Typically, the changes you'll be able to make will be small ones, such as tablecloths in a specific color or an

OPPOSITE: *Silver-painted bamboo chairs and ice-blue tablecloths create a serene setting in the elegant reception hall at a historic house and public garden in New York. The table linens reflect the bride's favorite color, blue.* ABOVE: *Twinkling white lights impart a magical aura to wedding receptions both indoors and out. Here, tiny lights are woven among the vines in a grape arbor, casting a soft glow on guests below.*

abundance of candles. Fresh flowers are a simple way to imbue any space with country style. A large floral arrangement might greet guests as they arrive, centerpieces can coordinate with your bridal bouquet, and floral details can even adorn chair backs if space allows. Ask whether the restaurant works with a particular florist exclusively or if you can hire your own.

To find the restaurant best suited to your needs, think first of places you already know and love. If none comes to mind, or if none can comfortably accommodate your guests, ask friends and colleagues for recommendations or check local restaurant reviews. Be sure that whichever place you choose is one you've dined at more than once, so you know without a doubt that the food, décor, and service are consistently first rate. Your initial meeting will likely be with the establishment's manager or event planner to discuss general details about renting the space, what dates and times are available, and the like. Once you have narrowed the search, meet with the chef to come up with a wedding menu. In most cases, the menu will be a variation of the food usually served at the restaurant, with input from you regarding your favorite dishes, flavors, and ingredients. Ask about desserts as well. The pastry chef on staff can usually make the wedding cake; there may be an extra charge if you plan to use an outside baker. Finally, find out if unique party favors can be created for your guests, such as specially printed menu cards or small boxes of pastries or truffles made by the pastry chef.

Bottom Line: **A restaurant is the right location for you if you want to treat your guests to a memorable meal in a sentimental setting and if you look forward to working with an event specialist to simplify the planning on your end.**

Loft

With its high ceilings, large windows, and white walls, a loft is like blank canvas onto which a bride and groom may paint their ideal vision of a wedding celebration. Because the spaces are often completely stark, they are best suited to couples with a creative eye or a talented wedding designer. Flowers, flowing fabrics, topiaries, paper lanterns, and twinkling lights are just a few of the decorative elements that can be used to transform the raw space. Anyone up for the challenge will find great reward in the finished results.

If you plan to hold both your ceremony and reception in a loft, you'll need to designate and decorate areas for each event. For ceremonies, look for eye-catching architectural details or a sunny window with a lovely arch that may serve as a focal point. Position a flower-covered arch or a pair of flower-filled urns near the focal point, and then create an aisle leading to it with chairs and a length of carpet. Receptions can take over the entire loft. Depending on the overall square footage, you can carve out separate spots for cocktails, dinner, and dancing.

With myriad details to keep track of, the aid of a wedding planner can be invaluable when marrying in a loft. Sometimes lofts have event planners on staff, especially if the spaces are frequently rented for weddings. Ask to see photographs of past weddings, if available, to spark ideas for your own celebration. Ask about caterers, bakers, and florists who have worked in the space before, and schedule tastings and consultations to see if they might be right for your wedding.

Lofts can be found in both big cities and small towns. Often, they are located in renovated warehouses and textile mills that now house shops, artists' studios, and open space for private parties. If you don't know of any lofts near you, call your local chamber of commerce or ask local caterers and florists who may have worked on an event at such a spot. Schedule a tour of any loft you're considering for your wedding to be sure the level of renovation is pleasing to your eye. Some places are expertly finished with well-appointed restrooms and closets for checking coats, while others are a bit more rough.

𝓑ottom line: **A loft is the right location for your wedding if you have a creative eye and you are up for the challenge of transforming a raw space into an oasis.**

To bring the outdoors in at a ceremony or reception, decorate with small clusters of flowers secured with satin or grosgrain ribbon.

2

Designing Your Day

From invitations that create a sense of anticipation to parting gifts that let your guests know how much you appreciated their presence, these are the thoughtful details that personalize a wedding and make the celebration uniquely you. In this chapter, we'll discuss the many ways you can infuse your wedding with your own distinctive style.

Choose a Theme

It may be a favorite color, a favorite flower, or a vacation spot you visited with your fiancé. It may be a children's book whose illustrations enchanted you when you were young. It may even be a favorite song. Whatever sparks your imagination, having a theme for your wedding creates a sense of continuity in the preparations and the celebration itself. Your theme doesn't have to influence every aspect of the wedding but should be used just enough to be noticed and to make the day more meaningful to you. If your favorite color is blue, for example, you might choose pale blue stationery for your invitations, dress your bridesmaids in a deep teal, and set the tables with blue-and-white china. Love forget-me-nots? Work them into your bridal bouquet, find thank-you notes with pictures of the petite blooms, and send guests home with seed packets so they can plant the flowers in their gardens and forever think of you. It can be fun to imagine all the different ways you might introduce your theme throughout the day.

ABOVE AND LEFT: *At this barn reception, long tables are dressed simply: white linens and casual clusters of flowers. The pig decoration at the center of the table is a playful touch; each table is decorated with a different animal. At each place setting, good-luck horseshoe favors await guests.* OPPOSITE FAR LEFT: *Inspired by a favorite childhood picture book, one bride and groom carried the theme through to the party favors—papier-mâché boxes embellished with illustrations from the storybook and filled with pastel candy hearts.* OPPOSITE NEAR LEFT: *An appreciation for the graphics of cigar-box labels sparked the idea for these accordion-fold wedding invitations, which were mailed to guests in CD cases with cigar-box seals.*

ᴄ᷀ᴄ᷀ Wedding Stationery ᴄ᷀ᴄ᷀

Through your stationery, you can connect one-on-one with each guest, making them feel welcome and appreciated. Invitations and save-the-date cards offer friends and family their first glimpse of what's to come; thank-you notes give you the opportunity to tell each guest how much it meant to you to have them share your special day.

While pure white paper with an embossed, cursive font is a timeless choice that will never go out of style, a country wedding gives you license

ABOVE: *Incorporating imagery from the garden on the wedding stationery is a natural choice for a country wedding—from invitations and thank-you notes to programs and menu cards. Here, delicate fern fronds grace a wedding program. If your printer does not have an illustration you love, look through design books or enlist the aid of an artistic friend.* OPPOSITE: *If you're having trouble finding just the right border or illustration for your invitations or wedding stationery, consider drawing one yourself or enlisting the aid of an artistic friend. A quaint hand-drawn botanical border outlines this invitation for a rehearsal dinner held in the bride and groom's garden.*

to be as creative as you like. Consider paper with a hint of color—powder blue, soft brown, sage green—or a thick, handmade feeling. Study old-fashioned fonts, talk to a calligrapher, or enlist the aid of a friend with clear, distinctive handwriting to create an eye-catching look for your stationery.

Decorative elements can beautify (and unify) your invitations and thank-you cards. If you've chosen a theme for your wedding, here is a great place to showcase it. If it's a particular flower you're focusing on, incorporate an illustration of the bloom on the cards. A small drawing of the location of your wedding, whether it's a hotel, an inn, or a barn, can also work well.

Once a very formal affair, a wedding as well as the rules surrounding the wording on the wedding stationery have loosened over the years. Many couples choose to include the names of both sets of parents on their invitations, while others extend the invitation using only their own names, adding the line "along with their families." Whatever you feel most comfortable with will be the right wording for you. Likewise, thank-you notes once featured the bride's new married name. These days you are just as likely to see only the first names of the bride and groom or just the last name (or single initial) if the bride will be taking her husband's name.

Kara Larson & John Koenig
4065 NORTHEAST NINTH
PORTLAND, OREGON
97212

please join us for a

Celebration Dinner

when   THURSDAY, AUGUST 2nd
7:00 pm

where   KARA & JOHN'S GARDEN
4065 NE NINTH

rsvp   PLEASE CALL 503-287-3465
BY JULY 25th, THANK YOU

please call for directions or visit mapquest.com

ALEXIS and REY

ALEXIS KELLY & REY ANDRADE

TOGETHER WITH THEIR FAMILIES INVITE YOU

TO JOIN THEM IN CELEBRATING THEIR MARRIAGE

FRIDAY, THE TENTH OF OCTOBER

TWO THOUSAND AND EIGHT

CEREMONY AT SIX O'CLOCK IN THE EVENING

AT THE BARR MANSION, AUSTIN, TEXAS

COCKTAILS, DINNER AND DANCING TO FOLLOW

October Tenth 2008

~ Programs ~

A wedding program serves a number of purposes. It identifies members of the wedding party, and lets guests follow along with the order of readings, music, and vows during the ceremony. What's more, it acts as a keepsake so that guests can look up the readings on their own, if they wish, or access the special songs you've chosen. Programs don't have to be as formal as wedding stationery (although they certainly can be) in terms of thick papers and embossed writing or calligraphy. You can type a simple schedule of the ceremony in a pretty font on your computer and have it copied onto colored paper. Include the names of all the participants who will be reading or playing music as well as their relationship to the bride or groom so your guests will know the significance of each person's contribution.

While programs are not mandatory, they can make guests feel more involved in your wedding, and they are a lovely way to help guests follow the ceremony, especially if the proceedings include traditions that might not be familiar to everyone attending. In addition, the design of the program is another opportunity to showcase your theme for the day.

OPPOSITE: *Your invitations offer guests their first taste of what your special day will be like, so feel free to be as creative as you choose. Sheet music, bluebirds, evocative fonts, and a length of twine distinguish this one-of-a-kind design.* ABOVE: *Along with a wedding program, custom-designed tissues placed on each guest's seat are a thoughtful and memorable touch.*

BELOW TOP: *To create memorable place settings, incorporate an item related to the season or location of your wedding. At this beach wedding, individual menus are decorated with dried sea stars tied with raffia.* BELOW BOTTOM: *Wedding programs tied with delicate ribbons are arranged in a wide ceramic bowl. Other receptacles that could hold programs in a similarly stylish fashion include a large rustic basket and, for outdoor ceremonies, a weathered birdbath or wheelbarrow.* RIGHT: *Tiny potted plants prevent place cards from blowing away in a breeze. Hiring a calligrapher to inscribe place cards (and perhaps embellish them with a small botanical design) will give your wedding stationery a personal touch.* OPPOSITE: *Single blooms in small vases act as table assignments and party favors. The rows of flowers also make an eye-catching display when guests arrive at the reception.*

Do It Yourself

Many country brides are also crafters, skilled bakers, or creative floral designers, so it's only natural that they would want to include these most personal of details throughout their wedding. Projects can be highly intricate or simple enough for anyone to complete. No matter your skill level, guests will be enchanted by your handcrafted designs.

INVITATIONS AND OTHER WEDDING STATIONERY. If you have calligraphy skills or pretty handwriting, you can use this talent to create place cards, menus, and even, time permitting, invitations. Your local stationer or art supply store can provide you with guidance and an abundance of paper stock and invitation templates to work with. Alternatively, an artful rubber stamp and an inkpad in a color that coordinates well with your wedding hues can transform plain card stock into personalized stationery. You can also embellish any card that has a black-and-white stamped image or line drawing with a touch of colored pencil or watercolor.

CENTERPIECES. If you have an affinity for floral arranging, simple centerpieces are another element of the wedding that you can create yourself. Using flowers that complement your wedding's signature hues, you can design charming centerpieces using vases, baskets, or colorfully embellished tin cans.

DRESSES. The truly industrious bride may make her own wedding gown—choosing her pattern, fabrics, and decorative details with the greatest of care. Or, you can put your sewing skills to work on an existing dress—perhaps one that you've inherited or purchased at a vintage dress shop—with a few simple alterations. Skilled seamstresses who'd rather buy their dream dress might still try their hands at pretty designs for their flower girls.

GIFTS. Handcrafted or homemade favors are another place to showcase your talents (and save on expenses). Personal touches are always memorable, and the options are boundless, ranging from sewing simple drawstring bags and filling them with candy, baking cookies and decorating them with your monogram, or crafting small books filled with your favorite quotations about life and love.

PHOTO COLLAGES. If you'd like to share photographs of yourself and your fiancé, cover a large corkboard with pretty fabric or tulle and then pin a loving selection of photographs of you and your fiancé as children, as young adults, and as a couple. Include images with parents and siblings, such as snapshots taken on childhood vacations. Place the collage on the table with the guest book or at an easily accessible spot at the reception.

Handmade details—and a touch of something blue—add country charm to a wedding. To make this ring bearer's pillow, the four corners of a delicately embroidered handkerchief were folded over a small pillow and secured with needle and thread. A length of thin white ribbon holds the rings in place.

Recycle your flowers. Offer them to guests as they leave, reuse them if you're hosting a farewell brunch the morning after the wedding, or donate them to a local hospital or senior citizens center.

ABOVE: *Many brides choose to coordinate their own bouquet with their bridesmaids' arrangements. A case in point is this bridal bouquet (center). Roses, tulips, and hydrangea blossoms reflect the bride's favorite colors of pink and blue. Simple clusters of roses for the attendants mirror a similar pale-pink palette. Cabbage leaves act as a common thread that connects all three bouquets.*
OPPOSITE: *Even the simplest bouquet can have a stunning impact. Wonderfully fresh and pretty, this daisy bouquet exudes charm.*

Flowers

Variations on a theme—that is the secret of a beautiful, cohesive look for the flowers on your wedding day. Having a common thread through all the arrangements, from bouquets to boutonnieres to centerpieces, creates an overall impression that reflects your personal style. Begin with your bridal bouquet. This arrangement usually includes a bride's favorite flowers and colors. The bridal bouquet also tends to match the bride's personal style in her choice of wedding dress—a lush grouping of roses and trailing ivy would complement a romantic gown resplendent with ruffles and tulle, while a tight cluster of lilies-of-the-valley would pair well with a simple satin shift.

Once you've settled on a bridal bouquet you love, branch out from there. Bouquets for bridesmaids are often similar but smaller versions of the bridal bouquet. You might choose identical bouquets for all your attendants or vary the blooms somewhat; if the bridal bouquet is made up of flowers in a particular shade of pink, for instance, your attendants' bouquets might showcase lighter and darker shades of the hue.

Next, move on to centerpieces and large arrangements for serving tables and buffets. These, too, can draw upon colors and flowers similar to those found in the bridal bouquet.

Consider making each tabletop arrangement slightly different—guests will enjoy seeing the variations as they walk around the reception. If you need to cut corners on your floral budget, larger arrangements are good places to incorporate seasonal greens and decorative branches.

Survey your ceremony and reception sites to see what other places might benefit from floral decorations. Doorways, tent poles, and barn rafters are natural spots for garlands. Fill a weathered birdbath or garden urn with blooms and place it where your guests will arrive as a welcome. Nearly any spot can be beautified with the addition of flowers.

While there are no right or wrong flowers to use at a wedding, there may be seasonal or budget restrictions that will guide your choices. A good florist will help you decide on the best blooms for you. (To locate a florist whose style mirrors your own, see "Finding a Florist" on page 108.) Remember that country weddings convey casual elegance: Feel free to experiment with berries, foliage, or even colorful vegetables if they enhance a floral arrangement.

OPPOSITE: *A simple centerpiece brimming with brightly hued flowers can be just as distinctive as an elaborate one. Flower-filled baskets are evocative of country style, inexpensive, and, for the do-it-yourself bride, don't require expert skills.* ABOVE LEFT: *Resting on tables cloaked in blue matelasse with white embroidery, centerpieces of lilacs, peonies, dogwood, and ranunculus capture the spirit of the season at this May wedding.* ABOVE RIGHT: *A pretty detail for an outdoor wedding is a birdbath with floating fresh-cut flowers, like the cheerful daisies seen here. A birdbath can even serve as the focal point for the ceremony location.*

ABOVE LEFT: *Any blooms, whether elegant roses or humble garden flowers, look dramatic when clustered together. Here, a simple centerpiece was created by cutting the stems of pink snapdragons short and clustering them in a trio of antique silver cups.* ABOVE CENTER: *Vintage tin canisters or new examples with colorful designs are perfect for casual floral arrangements at country weddings. This whimsical design complements the bright-blue blooms it holds.* ABOVE RIGHT: *Silver Victorian-style tussie-mussie holders can be filled with blooms and tied to chair backs for a simple, decorative touch. To imitate the look, make paper cones using silver doilies and place florist's Oasis foam inside to hold flowers in place.* OPPOSITE: *Fragrant and beautiful, bouquets of roses, sweet peas, and lilacs display subtle tints of lavender and peach. The colors complement the soft beige of the bridesmaid dresses while the loose, carefree style of the arrangements is well suited to the rustic surroundings.*

OPPOSITE: *Spindle-back chairs with varying silhouettes await guests. Pastel hues unify the seating and add a playful look to the dinner table.* ABOVE: *Striking in their simplicity, blue-tinged canning jars filled with hydrangea blossoms decorated the dining tables at this outdoor reception. Brown-and-white gingham tablecloths add another layer of laidback country style.*

⌒ Table Settings ⌒

The way the tables are set at your wedding meal says as much about your taste as any other part of the celebration. You might prefer an understated style, with all white plates and silver candlesticks, or one that is highly personal, such as mismatched rose-patterned plates and garden ornament cupids set among the flowers. Shopping at antiques shops and flea markets is one way to pick up tabletop treasures that will personalize your settings. Antique watering cans or vintage florist baskets hold the flowers; vintage salt and pepper shakers can be conversation starters; ornate silver frames can hold menu cards on each table.

Before dishes, flowers, and accessories can even be set in place, tablecloths form the foundation of the table. Here, too, you can go with traditional white linen or something less common, such as a soft-pink damask or a solid color that coordinates with the main color of the wedding. In general, pale colors work best for weddings because they won't compete with patterned plates and floral arrangements. One tablecloth option that combines both rustic and formal elements is to lay lengths of burlap over the table and then cover it with thin white gauze or tulle.

Even the seemingly simple place card can benefit from a creative eye. Vintage postcards, black-and-white photographs, smooth river rocks, small flowerpots, and miniature pumpkins are just some of the things you can write guests' names on to designate their spots at the table. Be as imaginative as you please.

OPPOSITE: *Eye-catching table settings like this one are easy to recreate, because almost any color pairs well with white. Begin with white linens and white chairs. For a centerpiece, choose boldly colored flowering plants. Next, find cloth napkins that coordinate with the flowers (in this case, red) and fold and place them at each place setting between the flatware. A circle of votive candles and a sprinkling of color-coordinated flower petals provide the perfect finishing touch.* ABOVE: *Find inspiration in the garden when designing a reception table outdoors. Here, fern fronds are tucked into each napkin. Country weddings encourage unexpected color combinations, like the teal-blue bordered china set atop a brown tablecloth.*

ABOVE LEFT: *At the end of each long table in a barn, bread baked in the shape of a bow embellishes a garland of herbs, olive boughs, and figs. The choice of greenery was inspired by Tuscany, where the bride studied while in college. The crisp white table linens and simple wood folding chairs underscore the quiet beauty of the barn's interior.* **ABOVE RIGHT:** *In keeping with their Tuscan theme, the bride and groom chose a few long tables for their barn reception instead of the dozen or so round tables it would have taken to accommodate their guests. The long tables call to mind family-style meals in the Italian countryside and are in keeping with the casual spirit of the day. Strung from the rafters, paper lanterns and twinkling lights illuminate the tables below.* **OPPOSITE:** *Grapevine birds' nests filled with sugared almond "eggs" delight guests at one country wedding. The charming favors doubled as place cards.*

PART 2: DESIGNING YOUR DAY

OPPOSITE: *A calligrapher or friend with distinctive handwriting can help create pretty table numbers. The deep browns of the table and chairs at this garden reception as well as the neutral tones of the flowers, vases, and clear glass accessories make the entire arrangement seem as if it is part of the natural surroundings.* ABOVE AND LEFT: *Boxed favors serve as place cards at this outdoor wedding and add a touch of color to the simple table setting. Each box holds a ripe Star Crimson pear and a John Lennon quotation. White pillar candles in votive holders run the length of the table, providing a gentle glow as the evening wears on.*

ABOVE LEFT: *There are no rules governing the types of china that can be used at a country wedding, so feel free to play with the colors, patterns, and even ages of your plates. Here, two new dishes—one green and one white with pink dots—sit under an antique rose-print plate.* ABOVE RIGHT: *Once they had decided on a lobster picnic for their reception, one couple chose attractive lobster crackers as party favors their guests could use right away. Red-and-white gingham ribbons lend a festive air to each place setting and coordinate with the table's red-and-white theme.* RIGHT: *Think of ways that place cards can be used as party favors, like the miniature watering cans filled with flowers at this garden reception. Pinking sheers were used to create a simple zigzag edge around each guest's name.* OPPOSITE: *As a playful touch, one couple designates the chairs they will use at their reception. The brown lettering and brown ribbon that secures the signs complement the color scheme of the table settings. Bouquets of cheerful sunflowers offer pleasing contrast to the darker hues around the table.*

Collections

The objects you collect say so much about you—your interests, pastimes, and passions. Incorporating them into your wedding is a simple way to add a personal touch to the day's events. Collections of milk-glass vases, damask tablecloths, or silver napkin rings, for example, can be showcased on the dinner tables. Souvenir salt and pepper shakers from places you and your fiancé visited are another fun tabletop idea. Vintage aprons, beaded purses, and costume jewelry are just a few of the items that can be shared with your attendants to create a distinctive look. On buffet tables, supplement the serving pieces with yellowware bowls, ironstone pottery, or vintage baskets lined with cloth napkins. Guest books are often placed alone on a table; arrange a cluster of favorite pieces nearby, such as figurines, windup toys, or family photos set in antique frames. Entrust a friend or relative to collect your precious possessions at party's end so that nothing gets scooped up unintentionally by caterers and cleanup crews.

Cozy Nooks

Weddings are festive affairs where the energy of all the assembled guests is infectious. But as much as your friends and family revel in the joyful noise of cocktail hour or the flurry on the dance floor, they also enjoy the opportunity to catch up with people they may not have seen in a long time. To this end, it's a thoughtful touch to create cozy spots where guests can talk in small groups or reconnect one-on-one. The recipe is simple: Position a bench, two comfortable armchairs, or a small table surrounded by two to four chairs in a quiet corner off to the side of the main reception area. You may even find yourself stealing some time there with an old friend or your beloved.

The Wedding Cake

Gone are the days when a three-tiered cake with white icing and a traditional bride-and-groom topper were the wedding standard. Today's cakes are small works of art that express the individuality of each and every couple. Some people have always held a mental picture of their dream cake in their heads; others cannot even conceive of the decorative possibilities that are out there until they visit a baker and flip through photographs from past nuptials. Whichever category you fit into, finding the right baker is an important first step in the process. (See "Finding a Baker" on page 114.) From there, you can let your imagination run free.

One of the most popular options today is a cake decorated with fresh flowers. They might

OPPOSITE: *Fresh fruit and a darker palette than is usually associated with a wedding proved to be eye-catching choices for this three tiered wedding cake. Deep-red dahlias, figs, and concord and champagne grapes adorn the chocolate confection.*

be roses, daisies, or dahlias—whatever blooms you like best in whatever colors you prefer. There may be seasonal considerations to discuss with your baker, as well as practical ones in terms of which cut flowers will stay freshest on your cake. Rolled fondant generally works best with floral designs because it is easier to remove the blooms from the stiff surface when it is time to cut the cake. When it comes to the look of the cake, flowers can be clustered on the top tier or they may line each tier all the way down. They may even be placed in a more organic way, seeming to tumble down the sides of the cake and stream onto the table. Often, small fruits, delicate ivy, or other foliage is incorporated into the decoration, creating a lovely botanical effect. Edible flowers like sugared violets, pansies, and rose petals are another intriguing idea.

To achieve a beautiful floral design that won't wilt over the course of the day, many

ABOVE LEFT: *In a playful twist on tradition, a wedding cake is surrounded by clusters of buttercream-frosted cupcakes. Vintage two-tiered metal tables, sprinkled with wildflowers, serve as cake stands.* ABOVE RIGHT: *With red and white—a classic country color combination—as the theme of the day, this stunning confection took shape. Layers of scarlet roses separate tiers of lemon-raspberry wedding cake covered with dotted Swiss fondant and embellished with gingham ribbon.* OPPOSITE: *Flower girls decorate the cake table (draped in a vintage tablecloth) and the grass around it with colorful rose petals. If your cake-cutting ceremony will take place in open air and under a hot sun, be sure to keep the cake in the shade or indoors until you are ready to begin.*

couples opt for icing techniques over fresh blooms. Icing also allows bakers to depict any flower you like, even those that are not available to you owing to seasonal or budget restraints. Other decora-tive details that can be created with icing are latticework, fruit and berries, and flowing ribbons. For a truly one-of-a-kind look, creative bakers can even use icing to make your cake resemble a treasured family heirloom such as a grandmother's cameo or a porcelain tea set in a classic blue-and-white pattern.

All-white cakes are still an option, of course, and one that many people choose. But today it is common for couples to add a little something extra to the design if they are attracted to a white palette. Some choose a white-on-white texture: polka dots, pearl trim, tiny bows, or the look of handmade lace. White flowers, either fresh or made from icing, are a wonderful finishing touch.

Parting Gifts

Thoughtful party favors are a way to thank your guests for participating in your wedding. They needn't be flashy or expensive, just a simple token as a take-home souvenir of your special day. Edible treats are popular and easily accessible. You might choose regional delicacies (maple syrup, saltwater taffy, salsa) or something produced at the location of your wedding (a

handled bag filled with apples from a farm, for example, or a bottle of wine from a vineyard). A small sampling of sweets such as chocolate truffles, peanut brittle, or candied almonds is another delicious idea.

Gifts that can be planted in the garden are another option, and one that is especially well suited to a country wedding. Herbs in pots that bear each guest's name can be placed at each seat at the dinner tables, thereby acting as both place card and party favor. Seed packets of a favorite flower or herb are pretty and practical. Look for packets with decorative designs or embellish simpler ones with a length of thin satin ribbon. A fun idea for late-summer or fall weddings: Place a handful of spring bulbs in a large square of tulle and tie at the top with satin ribbon or raffia.

Small keepsakes are yet another category of parting gift you can explore. These might include picture frames, decorative boxes, or tiny crystal ornaments that cast rainbows when hung at the window. A holiday ornament that depicts something memorable about your wedding can become a treasured part of your guests' own family traditions: A barn or farmhouse ornament can be a lovely reminder of a farm wedding, a cluster of grapes for a vineyard wedding, a seashell or starfish for a beach wedding, and so on.

A fuchsia table runner picks up the bright hues of the floral arrangement. The color-coordinated party favors are tea canisters filled with aromatic tea—a nod to the bride's Asian heritage.

ABOVE LEFT: *Potted herbs set at each place enliven the table and serve as fragrant parting gifts for your guests. Depending on the time of year that your wedding takes place, you can give guests garden-ready favors appropriate to that season, such as pansies or petunias at an early-summer event or a selection of bulbs at a fall wedding.*
ABOVE RIGHT: *Chocolate bar party favors feature custom-designed labels. To find similar favors for your own wedding, inquire at local specialty chocolate shops or conduct an Internet search.*
BOTTOM RIGHT: *If holding your wedding in an area known for its local delicacies, consider incorporating them into your day. Here, petite bottles of maple syrup from a local farm double as place cards and party favors.* **OPPOSITE:** *Party favors that reflect the personal interests of the bride and groom are the most memorable. One couple who love to cook presented their guests with a collection of their favorite recipes in boxes tied with simple twine.*

good cookin'
with jenny and jc

The Ceremony Site

Whether you and your fiancé are exchanging vows in an open field, a hotel ballroom, or a house of worship, creating a decorative focal point for your ceremony underscores the significance of the precise spot where you will soon become husband and wife. A dramatic backdrop also has the added benefit of framing you, the groom, and your officiant in the photographs you will cherish for a lifetime. Flowers are the most common element that couples use to beautify their ceremony site. If an altar or archway is already in place, adorn it with blooms that reflect your personal style and coordinate with the other floral arrangements that were made for the day.

To create a focal point when one is lacking, erect a latticework archway and then weave in climbing vines, roses, or other blooms for a classic look. Flowing cloth or ribbons are other suitable embellishments for an archway. Another pretty option (and one that works especially well indoors) is to position a pair of beautiful urns at the end of an aisle and fill them with favorite flowers. As a finishing touch, tie small clusters of the same blooms to the chairs that line the aisle.

A final note about outdoor weddings: Some couples choose a wonderful old tree as a backdrop for their ceremony. If this idea intrigues you, consider decorating lower branches with ribbons or an artful arrangement of ornaments such as hearts, birds, or butterflies. For ceremonies held in your own garden or the garden of a close relative, you might consider planting a tree and marrying in front of it—you can watch the tree grow and mature as each year passes.

ABOVE: *Clusters of sunflowers decorate the four poles of a huppa that designates the ceremony site at a public garden. The bold yellow blooms stand out among the greenery of the garlands and the surroundings.* OPPOSITE: *A grassy bank beside a quiet pond is an ideal spot for an outdoor ceremony. To create a picture-perfect frame for their vows, this bride and groom decorated a wooden archway with clusters of white hydrangeas and soft greenery.*

OPPOSITE: *Guests stand at this outdoor ceremony held beneath towering oaks. This spontaneous and informal arrangement works well for short ceremonies. Keep a few folding chairs on hand for any guests who may need to sit; attendants or guests can tote the chairs back to the reception site after the ceremony.* ABOVE LEFT: *Instead of throwing rice, guests greeted the newlyweds with bubbles blown from miniature Taittinger Champagne bottles.* ABOVE RIGHT: *Tiny bells placed inside pretty muslin bags were given to each guest at one autumn ceremony. When the bride and groom walked down the aisle, newly wed, guests shook the bells in unison.* LEFT: *A tray of white sand is a stylish display for bundles of sparklers designated for each guest. Swedish fish candy is attached to the base of each group of sparklers, helping to anchor them in the sand.*

～⌒ Directional Signs ⌒～

Clear directional signs are a must, especially if your wedding will take place on a farm or other location along a country road with few markers. Visit an art store to buy white or light-hued poster board and thick, dark markers or black paint with a few thin brushes. Pick up wire and a wire cutter at a hardware store to hang your signs. Make enough signs to mark at least two turns before your location as well as a welcome sign to let guests know that they have arrived. Smaller signs might lead guests toward parking or the coat check or warn them about steep slopes or rocky paths.

Clarity is the most important factor when making your signs, but if anyone you know has neat handwriting that is also playful and distinctive, enlist their aid. Hang signs early on the morning of your wedding so they are in place for your caterer, florist, and other vendors who will be arriving before your guests. Be sure all signs are firmly attached with wire so that they will not bend in the wind or blow away.

OPPOSITE: *More than 200 red 'Charlotte' roses—the bride's favorite variety—form a heart that greets guests at a wedding on a Pennsylvania farm. To create it, the bride (a floral designer) simply tucked the stems into a water-soaked heart-shaped Oasis form.* ABOVE: *Handwritten signs guide guests to the wedding and also greet them once they've arrived. Playful borders and swirling letters distinguish these signs, hung intentionally askew on a white picket fence to attain a carefree look.*

Something Old

Antiques and heirlooms can make a heartfelt statement in a modern-day wedding. Your "something old" might be your mother's dress or your grandmother's string of pearls. Brides without such wearable heirlooms can scour antiques shops, estate sales, and online auctions to find similar items. The following is a list of the most popular objects that brides and grooms search for.

WEDDING GOWNS. A wide range of antique and vintage fashions can be found, including high-necked Edwardian designs from the early 1900s, flapper-style dresses from the 1920s, and 1960s A-line shifts. Condition can often be a factor with old dresses; if one you love needs more than a few repairs, consider having it professionally restored. For referrals, contact the American Institute for Conservation of Historic and Artistic Works (aic.stanford.edu).

ACCESSORIES. Gloves, veils, shoes, handkerchiefs, purses, and prayer books are just a few of the items that today's brides are looking for. Delicate details are desirable, such as tiny pearl beads on gloves, wax flowers on shoes, or antique lace on a veil. The degree of ornamentation on anything old should match your overall style for the day.

JEWELRY. Tiaras, earrings, strings of pearls, lockets, and even wedding bands and engagement rings are sought after. In the case of engagement rings, many brides appreciate the uncommon settings and distinctive look of the stones on older rings. Jewelry auctions are great places to find exquisite examples from years past.

CAKE TOPPERS. Antique and vintage cake toppers have become hot collectibles. Styles range from fanciful Victorian designs with cupids and flowers to bride-and-groom kewpie dolls from the 1920s. Even simple and elegant examples from the 1950s are in demand. Among the rarest on the market are World War II–era toppers that feature military grooms.

BRIDAL PARTY GIFTS. Cufflinks, brooches, silver pillboxes, bud vases, picture frames, and pretty plates are always enchanting and are often one-of-a-kind. Gifts from the past are especially appropriate for your bridesmaids and groomsmen if you are known for your love of antiques and collectibles: Treasures from the past will capture your personality more than anything you can find in a retail shop.

OPPOSITE: *Collections can add a wonderful, personal touch to a wedding. Here, the bride's prized milk-glass vases span the length of her reception table—each filled with a different grouping of roses. The tall hobnail example was a wedding gift the bride's mother received at her wedding.*

A Wedding Primer

You've settled on the location. You've chosen your theme. You can picture your wedding day exactly as you'd like it to be. Now how do you turn that vision into reality? In this chapter, we'll lead you through the process and tell you all you need to know.

Setting a Budget

There are so many variables involved in planning a wedding that it can be difficult to predict an exact cost at the outset. Nonetheless, it's wise to agree on a ballpark figure that represents what you and your fiancé feel comfortable spending, or at least to set a ceiling amount you don't wish to go above. Today it's common for couples to cover some or all of their wedding expenses. Whichever arrangement works best for you, the following considerations will help you reach a realistic budget to achieve your ideal wedding day.

Let your location be your guide. Not only does your choice of location set the tone for the look of your wedding, it also acts as a baseline for your budget. Once you know your rental fees for a reception in a hotel or botanical garden or the cost of raising a tent in your parents' backyard or on your uncle's farm, subtract that amount from your overall budget to determine how much you've got to work with for the rest of the celebration.

Where do you want to splurge? Decide what's most important to you, whether it's an abundance of orchids, a menu that could rival the finest restaurant, or a swing band you can dance to all night. Once you settle on the one or two areas you feel strongest about, you can cut corners elsewhere in the budget to make it all come together.

To save money, be flexible. One of the best ways to create your dream wedding for less is to consider off-peak times in terms of season, day of the week, and time of day. Saturday nights in fair-weather months from May through October are the most popular; reserving a Friday evening or Sunday afternoon, or an event held in the late fall through early spring are sure ways to reduce costs from the get-go. A reception venue that has tables, chairs, and linens on hand (rather than needing to rent them) is another option for the frugal bride.

Compare and negotiate. Before making any decisions about a service provider such as a baker, florist, or caterer, meet with more than one to compare prices and design options. The

Green TIP

Not only is candlelight romantic, it's energy efficient, too. Look for soy candles—they come in all shapes, sizes, and colors, and they're eco-friendly because they're made from a renewable resource.

overall cost shouldn't be your only motivator, however. Choose the person with whom you feel most comfortable, whose taste is like your own, and who also can best accommodate your budget. Don't be afraid to inquire, politely, about ways to lower your bill.

LEFT: *Finding out what flowers are in bloom at the time of your wedding is a good way to create striking seasonal displays. Sunflowers were plentiful at the time of this summer wedding in New Hampshire; large bunches of them were cut short and placed in terra-cotta garden pots.* ABOVE: *Using the bride's favorite color for inspiration, one florist created bridesmaids' bouquets in varying shades of pink, from palest seashell to deepest fuchsia. Here, velvety garden roses rest against a simple bed of cabbage leaves.*

Planning Boards and Notebooks

From the moment you become engaged, it's prudent to pick one spot to consolidate all your ideas and inspirations regarding your wedding. One stylish option is a planning board positioned over your desk. Find an attractive bulletin board or make one by covering a plain corkboard with pretty fabric. Indulge in decorative pushpins to hang pictures of wedding gowns, fabric swatches for bridesmaid dresses, business cards for bakers and florists, and the like. Another idea is a wedding notebook. Choose a three-ring binder and place folders inside, one for each aspect of your day: ceremony, flowers, reception, music, and so on. Keep a folder or sturdy envelope in your purse to collect ideas during the day, then transfer everything to your board or notebook in the evening.

Hiring a Wedding Planner

If your budget allows, it's worthwhile to consider a wedding planner. The best planners are extremely organized people who will oversee all the details of your wedding, from finding and reserving a great location to seeing that everything is ordered, delivered, set up, and taken down again. Planners have a databank of wedding resources and service providers at their fingertips, and they can help you sort through the numerous florists, caterers, musicians, and photographers in your town. They can frequently negotiate better prices along the way thanks in part to their ongoing relationships with the professionals in their field. Finally, wedding planners are often creative thinkers who not only help you identify your ideal wedding style but also devise innovative ideas to make your vision come to life.

To find a wedding planner in your area, begin by asking family and friends for recommendations. You can also conduct an Internet search of wedding planners in your town, county, or state. Once you have a few names, call them to schedule an initial meeting. Ask planners how long they have been in this line of work and how many weddings they have organized. Talk a bit about your ideas for your wedding and see if the planner seems enthusiastic about the possibilities of a country wedding. There should be an instant connection on a personal level between you and your wedding planner; you will be spending a good deal of time with that person over the coming months as you begin one of your life's momentous journeys. Before making a final decision, be sure to get names of past clients to call for references.

Make It Fun!

Let's face it—planning a wedding can be stressful. Too often we forget to enjoy the flurry of preparations and the sense of anticipation leading up to one of the happiest days of our lives. Be sure to schedule some relaxing, some laughter, and some silliness along the way.

PACK A PICNIC. When scouting outdoor locations, bring along a delicious lunch and a blanket to spread out on the grass. Stop by a gourmet shop in the morning and treat yourself to out-of-the-ordinary snacks and drinks.

LET THEM EAT CAKE. Bringing friends to a cake tasting is a wonderful outing and a good way to get input from trusted pals on which type of cake you should choose. Limit your group to no more than four people and call ahead to let the baker know how many are coming.

GO WINE TASTING. This is a must if you and your fiancé are thinking about getting married at a vineyard. But it can also be fun for you to attend tastings in local wine shops to become familiar with the regions and flavors you like best, so you'll know which wines you'd like to serve at your wedding.

VISIT A FLOWER FARM. The purpose of this trip can be either to get inspiration for the types of flowers you want your florist to use or to gather armloads of blooms so that you and your friends can make your own bouquets and table arrangements. Don't forget a camera (you might even want your photographer along) because opportunities for beautiful pictures will abound.

TAKE A YOGA CLASS. Deep breathing and relaxation techniques will definitely come in handy as the big day approaches. You might even plan a private class for your bridal party the morning of your wedding, before everyone begins getting dressed.

INDULGE AT A SPA. Whether you visit a day spa with friends for a bachelorette party or schedule a visit from a masseuse on the morning of your wedding, spa services are a sure way to relax and refocus your energy. One note: Don't schedule facials too close to your big day, in case your skin does not react well. Three days to a week in advance is best.

ABOVE LEFT: *Wedding programs and paper cones filled with flower petals rest on pretty, patterned seat cushions. At the end of the ceremony, guests showered the couple with the petals as the newlyweds made their way up the aisle.* above RIGHT: *One couple who are film buffs wrote out the names of their wedding party as cast members— a fun (and informative) detail for their guests. A similar sign could easily be produced with black poster board and a white paint pen or black chalkboard paint and plain white chalk (both available in art stores). An easel is a practical way to prop up the sign at eye level.*

PART 3: A WEDDING PRIMER

LEFT: *A vintage handkerchief embroidered with a blue monogram of the bride's first initial wrapped the stems of her bridal bouquet. Vintage hankies can be pretty and practical accessories at a wedding—they can be your "something old" or, as in this case, "something blue."* BELOW: *Table assignments "grow" from a collection of moss-filled briefcases and vanity boxes. Scouring local thrift shops, flea markets, and antiques malls is a good way to find similar cases that have a bit of age to them.*

OPPOSITE: *Rustic baskets adorned with blossoms and ribbons are ideal receptacles for flower petals. The sizes and styles of the baskets need not match precisely as long as the decorations used on each are similar. Floral head wreaths are timeless accessories for the youngest members of the wedding party.* ABOVE LEFT: *Suspending rings from a length of pretty ribbon is a good way to keep them together before the ceremony. These antique ring designs were the "something old" for one couple married on an Oregon vineyard. Whether family heirlooms or antique-shop treasures, old rings can be resized or set with new stones quite easily.* ABOVE RIGHT: *One couple's floral theme carried over to the dessert table, where cupcakes with sunflower frosting were arranged on a pretty tiered stand. Red lanterns add a punch of color during the day and promise atmospheric lighting when evening falls.*

ABOVE: *A horse-drawn carriage is one of the most romantic ways for a bride to arrive at her wedding. The gentle clip-clop of hooves also heightens the sense of anticipation guests feel as they try to catch their first glimpse of the bride.* OPPOSITE: *Antique and vintage cars are a stylish way to arrive at and depart from your wedding. Convertibles are especially picture-perfect. Inquire at local historical societies to find out about antique car clubs in your area that might rent nostalgic models for special events.*

⌐◦ Arriving in Style ◦⌐

Stretch limousines are an inherently practical way to bring bridal attendants, parents, and grandparents to and from the wedding. But for the bride and groom, there are a number of out-of-the-ordinary options that you might consider. A horse and carriage is one romantic idea. The gentle clip-clop of hooves heightens the anticipation of guests waiting to catch their first glimpse of the bride. To find a horse and carriage, contact local stables, ask a wedding planner, or check the classified ads in a local paper. Meet with the driver and see the carriage before making any decisions; it can also be helpful to ask to speak with someone who has used the service before.

Driving up to your wedding in an antique or vintage car is another idea that captures the imagination. A vintage white Rolls Royce is a popular choice with many couples, but many other styles from the past can also turn heads, like a vintage pickup for a farm wedding or a baby-blue 1950s tailfin model that matches the color of the bridesmaids' dresses. Check your local yellow pages, do an Internet search, or inquire at your local historical society to find antique or classic car clubs in your area and then call to see if they rent cars for special occasions. Some traditional limousine services also have

vintage cars on hand for weddings, so it's worthwhile to ask companies near you.

Even an everyday convertible—whether yours or a friend's—can be transformed into a stylish mode of transportation, provided it is in new or like-new condition. Clean and wax the car shortly before the wedding and park it in a garage or under a cover until the big day. On the morning of your wedding, decorate the car with streamers, garlands, or balloons and enjoy the waves and well-wishes you will undoubtedly receive from pedestrians and other drivers on the road.

Green TIP

Instead of throwing rice (which is harmful to the birds that swoop down to eat it), have guests shower you with flower petals or blow soap bubbles as you leave the ceremony.

Finding a Florist

Your ideal florist should have a style you admire— a style that matches your own—and a genuine interest in your personal vision for your wedding. To find someone you trust, start by asking friends, family, and colleagues for recommendations. You can also look up florists in your town in the yellow pages or online, then visit their shops to see if you feel a connection to the arrangements you see there.

Once you have settled on a few people, call to arrange face-to-face meetings to discuss the possibilities for your wedding. Bring pictures of arrangements you like, fabric swatches from bridesmaid dresses, and anything else that will help the florist understand your taste. Ask to see the florist's portfolio of flowers created for other weddings and, if you like what you see, ask to speak with former clients or read letters of recommendation the florist may have on hand. Don't be afraid to visit a florist you think might be too expensive for your budget. The finest and best floral designers will help you focus on what's most important to you—an exquisite bouquet, perhaps—and devise ways to cut costs in other places to create a beautiful overall look for the day.

When you make your decision, visit your ceremony and reception sites together with your florist. A written contract should outline all aspects of the day, from the bouquets, table and altar arrangements, and other floral decorations. The contract should list all costs and also a delivery schedule. Touch base with your florist two weeks before your wedding to reconfirm all the specifics and your delivery dates and times. If you have any last-minute changes to make, contact your florist as soon as possible to avoid additional charges. It's also worthwhile to ask if the florist or an assistant will be available on your wedding day in case there are any last-minute emergencies.

Green TIP

Choose flowers that are in season and grown locally to avoid the truck or plane transportation that would be required to ship out-of-season blooms.

ABOVE LEFT: *To free their hands, bridesmaids at this outdoor wedding fastened their brightly colored bouquets of roses and dahlias to their arms using coordinating satin ribbon.* ABOVE RIGHT: *Leaves and berries are uncommon yet attractive additions to a traditional boutonniere.*

OPPOSITE: *Delphiniums, roses, and grapevines grace a latticework arbor under which one couple wed in the bride's parents' backyard. Garden urns filled with trailing ivy underscore the symmetry of the scene.* ABOVE LEFT: *A moss-covered vintage birdbath became an ideal receptacle for a lively combination of 'Sensation' roses, 'Apricot Beauty' tulips, deep red echinacea pods, and bright green chili peppers. The arrangement was positioned at the edge of a field to greet guests as they walked towards the site where one couple would exchange vows on a sunny summer day.* ABOVE RIGHT: *In addition to floral arrangements in traditional places (on the dinner and serving tables, on the altar or ceremony site), set some in unexpected spots to surprise and delight your guests. Here, a weathered wrought-iron chair supports a creative combination of lavender roses, baby eggplants, and thistle that grows wild on a New Hampshire farm where the wedding took place.*

RIGHT: *Sometimes a simple twist on tradition can make a wedding memorable. At one backyard wedding in rural Connecticut, appetizers were served picnic-style from the tailgate of a 1948 Ford F1 pickup. Blue-and-white checkered tablecloths complement the arrangement. Vintage folding chairs are set around the food in an informal manner, inviting guests to linger and chat.* BELOW LEFT: *Galvanized metal tubs filled with ice make ideal receptacles for beer and sodas at a reception. Bottles of local microbrew beer fill this oval design.* BELOW RIGHT: *Serving drinks in handled canning jars adds old-fashioned flair to a country wedding. The raspberry lemonade seen here is both thirst-quenching and pleasing to the eye.*

Finding a Caterer

There was a time when the food served at a wedding was standard fare: a selection of time-tested appetizers and two or three entreés from which to choose, such as chicken, fish, or filet mignon. Today, more and more couples are choosing inventive menus with dishes that trigger fond memories like a vacation in Tuscany, a shared love of Cuban cuisine, or a grandmother's cooking. Ideally you want to find a caterer who will take personal cues like these and blend them with his or her own signature style to make your wedding dinner one of the highlights of the day.

As with florists, you can find caterers by asking people you know for recommendations. If you've recently (or even not so recently) attended a wedding or other catered affair and enjoyed the meal, ask the host for a reference. Some reception locations such as a hotel, inn, or botanical garden may have on-site catering or an exclusive contract with one company. This simplifies your search, to be sure, but you'll want to schedule a tasting before committing to the site to make certain that the food prepared is to your liking.

Make appointments to meet with potential caterers soon after booking your location. Like popular wedding venues, sought-after caterers fill up their calendars far in advance. At these initial meetings, share details about the size and style of your wedding as well as your food preferences. Ask caterers how many weddings they have done and ask to see past menus. Talk about any special dishes your guests might require, such as a vegetarian entrée or a guaranteed kid-pleaser. As with the other service providers for your wedding, you want to find a caterer with whom you feel comfortable, someone who listens well and comes up with ideas that intrigue and delight you.

When you find that person, plan a tasting that lets you and your fiancé sample the entire day's menu, from hors d'oeuvres and appetizers to entreés and dessert, if you will be offering other sweets in addition to the wedding cake. You should also be able to taste the wine and cham-pagne that will be served with each course. Ask to see what place setting options are available, and, to get a better sense of what the final visual effect will be, ask ahead of time for several to be prepared for you.

In addition to the size of your guest list, the ingredients you choose, and the number of courses you plan to have, other factors that can affect catering costs include how large your wait staff will be and what items will need to be rented. Most hotels and reception halls have essentials on hand for hosting a dinner, such as tables, chairs, china, linens, silverware, and glasses. Farms, lofts, and backyards will need all these things brought. Ask about the benefits and comparative costs of a buffet meal versus a formal sit-down dinner. A written agreement should outline all costs and should also include specifics as to time and place for delivery and set up. Ask if a manager will be on-site at your wedding to oversee the preparation and serving of food and if this service is included in the overall fee or at an additional charge. Touch base with your caterer about two weeks before your wedding to confirm all details.

~ Finding a Baker ~

There is no sweeter symbol of beginning your new life together than the cutting of the wedding cake. With so many design options available today, cakes have become small works of art. (For ideas, see "The Wedding Cake" on page 80). That's why finding a baker who can make your vision come to life is so essential.

You may already have a favorite pastry shop in your town that also makes wedding cakes. If you don't know of one, ask friends for suggestions. Wedding planners, caterers, and florists may be able to recommend someone as well. Call to arrange a meeting and tasting ten to twelve months before your wedding. Ask if there

will be a fee for the consultation and how many people can accompany you. The bride and groom often attend together, but it can also be fun to bring your mother or a small group of friends. No more than four people should attend a tasting.

At the initial meeting, a baker will want to know about the size of your guest list, the theme of the wedding, and the types of flowers or colors that will be used. The season in which your wedding will be held and whether it will be an outdoor or indoor affair will also be of interest, as these facts may affect your choice of filling, icing, and decoration. Look at photographs of other cakes the baker has designed and ask for references from past clients.

OPPOSITE: *Pretty cupcakes are a fun dessert option. A single icing flower on top of each confection can be color-coordinated with the bridal bouquet. Some couples serve cupcakes in addition to the cake; others choose them in place of a cake, arranging dozens of cupcakes on a tiered stand to mimic the look of a traditional tiered wedding cake.* LEFT: *Dotted Swiss blue fondant blankets a four-tiered chocolate cake. On the top, a fondant ribbon secures a bouquet of stephanotis crafted from sugar, the flower the bride's mother carried on her own wedding day.*

tract should clearly list all of the specifics about the cake, including the date and time of delivery or pickup. Check in a few weeks before your wedding to confirm all details with your baker.

Some industrious brides choose to bake their own wedding cake. Others have generous friends or family who offer to make the confection for them. Either scenario adds a sentimental, homespun touch to a country wedding. In general, homemade cakes are best for smaller weddings, especially at-home celebrations where the cake can be baked on the premises and not have far to travel. Invest in the best baking supplies and freshest ingredients before you begin and always plan a test run, baking a smaller version of the wedding cake to test the recipes for the cake, filling, and icing. Unless the person making the cake is a skilled baker able to create icing flowers and intricate decorations, consider placing fresh or sugared flowers on top or around the base of the cake. A vintage cake topper and rose petals scattered around the base of the cake make another beautifully simple decoration.

The price of a wedding cake is generally based on the number of guests it will need to serve and the extent of decoration you desire. You'll also want to find out if delivery and set up of the cake are included in the price or if there will be an extra charge involved. Will someone be on hand to cut the cake or will that task fall to the caterer or even a family member? A written con-

～ Finding a Photographer ～

Beautiful photographs preserve your wedding memories for a lifetime, so your choice of a photographer is a vital one. There are two main types of wedding photography. One is a more traditional portrait style, the other a more informal approach that seeks to document the day with candid shots and details such as close-ups of the bride's bouquet, a place card on a dinner plate, or a handwritten sign welcoming guests to the reception. Before you meet with any photographers, you should know which style you prefer. This will help you narrow your search.

Most wedding photographers have Internet sites these days, so conduct an online search for wedding photographers in your town or the wider metropolitan area, in addition to asking friends and family for recommendations. On their Internet sites, photographers commonly post condensed albums of the weddings they have shot. View these albums to get a sense of each photographer's style and to see if it matches your own vision. If you like what you see, arrange an interview.

As important as a photographer's past work is the rapport you feel with the photographer. After all, this is a person who is going to be with you throughout the day, from the time you are getting dressed for the ceremony until the time

you leave your reception. The photographer should make you feel comfortable and should listen with interest to your vision for your wedding. Whether or not the photographer is easy to work with is a question to ask prior clients, something you should certainly do before booking a photographer. At this initial meeting, you should also discuss costs. Ask whether the photographer will work alone or have an assistant along. Ask if there are overtime charges, when you can expect the proofs, and how you will go about ordering prints and organizing an album. If you want engagement shots or bridal portraits, now is also the time to ask about those.

Once you settle on someone you like, set up another meeting to run through the particulars of your wedding—go over where it will be held, what types of shots you want, and if there are particular people you don't want to be left out. Ask if the photographer has worked at your ceremony and reception venues before; if the answer is no, consider touring the sites together so he or she can get a sense of what the day will be like and where to be positioned to capture the best images. All of this information should be included on a written contract. Check in with the photographer again about a month before the wedding to go over the details of your agreement and to be sure everything is in place.

OPPOSITE: *A sweet way to acknowledge guests who cannot be with you on your special day owing to travel restrictions or illness is to take a photograph that includes a message, as this couple did.*

Wedding Timeline

For the best chance to secure your first choice of location, florist, caterer, and other service providers, it's advisable to begin your wedding planning ten to twelve months in advance. Of course, this timetable can be condensed if you are marrying at home or on a family farm, or to accommodate your own schedule.

10 TO 12 MONTHS BEFORE

Set a date.

Determine your budget.

Hire a wedding planner, if you decide to use one.

Complete your guest list.

Choose the locations(s) of your ceremony and reception.

Choose your bridesmaids and groomsmen.

Decide on the wedding theme.

Begin interviewing caterers.

Begin interviewing florists.

Begin interviewing musicians.

Begin interviewing photographers.

Begin interviewing bakers for the wedding cake.

Begin looking at dress designs.

Begin looking at invitations.

Send an engagement announcement to your local newspaper and have an engagement photo taken, if you wish.

If creating a wedding Web site, begin the process and/or meet with the designer.

6 TO 9 MONTHS BEFORE

Book caterer.

Book florist.

Book musicians.

Book photographer.

Order the cake.

Order invitations.

Mail save-the-date cards.

Arrange for accommodations for out-of-town guests.

Choose an officiant and discuss your ceremony plans with him or her.

Reserve a tent, if needed.

Order wedding rings (and engravings, if needed).

Order wedding dress, veil, shoes, and other accessories and schedule dress fittings.

Order attire for groom, bridesmaids, and groomsmen, and schedule fittings.

Launch wedding Web site.

Register for gifts.

Begin making wedding night arrangements.

Begin making honeymoon arrangements.

3 MONTHS BEFORE

Book a hairdresser and makeup artist, if you choose to use them, and schedule a run-through.

Finalize menu with caterer.

Finalize details with florist.

Write or decide on wedding vows.

Choose readings for the ceremony, if needed.

Write and order wedding programs.

Confirm delivery dates for the wedding dress and wedding party attire.

Address and mail invitations.

Choose music for the ceremony and select a song list for the reception.

Order gifts for attendants and party favors for guests.

If making crafts for the wedding or to give as gifts, start them now.

Plan rehearsal and rehearsal dinner.

2 MONTHS BEFORE

Mail invitations for the rehearsal dinner.

Hire transportation for the bride, groom, and attendants (and guests, if needed).

Finalize ceremony and reception schedules.

1 MONTH BEFORE

Determine seating plan for reception.

Send a photography list and wedding schedule to the photographer; confirm details.

Get a marriage license.

Send wedding announcement to the newspaper.

2 WEEKS BEFORE

Confirm details with caterer.

Confirm details with florist.

Confirm details with musicians.

Confirm details with baker.

Confirm time of rehearsal and rehearsal dinner.

Pick up and try on dress, veil, shoes, and accessories.

Confirm wedding day schedule.

Contact guests who have not RSVP'd.

1 WEEK BEFORE

Confirm transportation details for the wedding party and guests.

Forward final head count to caterer.

Write place cards (if not ordering from stationer or calligrapher).

Confirm hair and beauty appointments.

Make or pick up directional signs for the wedding.

Confirm honeymoon arrangements.

THE DAY BEFORE

Give gifts to wedding party.

Rehearse ceremony.

Rehearsal dinner.

Hair and Makeup

A word about hair and makeup for a country wedding: Keep it natural. Avoid heavy makeup or shades you do not usually wear. Instead, opt for a slightly more made-up version of your normal routine. A foundation or tinted moisturizer is advisable to give your skin a balanced appearance, but skip the sunscreen if you will be photographed outdoors: sunscreen reflects light and makes skin appear lighter in pictures. Rice-paper blotting sheets (available in beauty supply stores and in the beauty aisle of many drugstores) are good to keep on hand to absorb shine throughout the day, without having to apply more makeup.

Your hair, too, should be kept simple. Up and away from the face is a classic style that will look timeless in photographs. Flowers in your hair—whether a wreath designed by your florist or simply a few blooms tucked into a bun—is another romantic look. Many brides arrange for a makeup artist and hairdresser to help them prepare for their wedding day. Ask for references from friends or relatives or inquire at your own salon. When meeting with a hair or makeup professional, bring a picture of your wedding dress and, especially for a hairdresser, your veil and any tiara or other headpiece you wish to wear. Be prepared to talk about your personal style and details about the style of your wedding. Arrange for a run-through of both hair and makeup before your wedding to be sure you are pleased with the way you look.

Attire

One of the wonderful things about a country wedding is the freedom to envision the day exactly as you wish—right down to the clothes that you, your fiancé, your wedding party, and your guests wear. Many brides opt for a traditional white gown even in a rustic setting, but the designs are often simple silhouettes with minimal embellishment. Other brides look for a pretty dress that is not a wedding dress per se, or they may decide on a color other than white: pale pink, sea green, or sky blue, for example. (That's one way to get your "something blue!") If your wedding will take place outdoors, you might consider an ankle-length dress instead of full length to avoid grass and mud stains, especially if there's any possibility of rain. The rule of thumb for any dress you choose is that it should make you feel beautiful and happy.

Dress options for bridal attendants have also expanded from what they once were. Gone are the long, pastel gowns that can be worn only

OPPOSITE: *Dramatic backdrops for wedding portraits abound on a farm. Look for weathered wood fences like this one, horses or sheep grazing in a meadow, a cornfield, colorful wildflowers, a big red barn, or a towering oak tree, to name just a few.*

once, and in their place are chic cocktail dresses in a range of stylish colors: champagne, chocolate brown, apple green. Many brides choose to coordinate the color of their attendants' dresses with the overall color theme of the day. Other brides are inspired by the hue of a favorite flower in their bridal bouquet, choosing either one color for all the dresses or a range of shades such as palest seashell pink to deepest coral. In a country setting, bridesmaids can even wear flowing, flowery dresses or other designs not necessarily intended for a wedding party. Include your bridesmaids in the planning process to be sure the dress is one they will feel enthusiastic about wearing at your wedding and at other events in the future. If there are differing opinions, however, remember that the final design decision is yours.

Even fashions for grooms and ushers have evolved over the years. While tuxedos are still the norm for traditional wedding attire, in a country wedding the look is oftentimes more casual. The groom and other men in the bridal party might choose classic suits in navy or tan, perhaps with coordinated ties in a color that matches the bridesmaid dresses or the bridal bouquet. The navy blazer over tan pants is another timeless look that is appropriate for

warm weather weddings in a country setting. Let your location and the overall style of the day be your guide.

Unless they are informed otherwise, most guests dress up for a wedding. Men will often wear regular business suits unless the invitation indicates that the event is black tie, in which case they will need to wear a tuxedo—their own or rented. If your wedding will be a decidedly more casual affair, with you wearing a garden-party dress instead of a wedding gown and the groomsmen in slacks and blazers, let your guests know by writing "country casual attire" on your invitation, or by including the nature of the celebration, such as "square dance in the barn to follow dinner." This will let guests know that while they should still dress nicely, they needn't don their fanciest attire or their highest heels. (Unless they want to, of course.)

OPPOSITE: *Wearing dresses designed by the bride and protected by vintage aprons, friends helped serve dinner at this vineyard wedding.*

OPPOSITE: *If no single wedding gown you find captivates you, consider working with a dress designer to create a unique design all your own. This vintage-inspired dress, designed by the bride, combines appliquéd raised florets, a scalloped hem, and a simple scoop neck.* ABOVE: *Cozy pashmina shawls are sensible and stylish accessories for outdoor weddings at times of the year when an afternoon or evening chill is a possibility. The shawls can also be thoughtful gifts from a bride to her attendants that they can use again and again.* LEFT: *Baby-blue Mary Janes are this bride's "something blue." Other ways to incorporate something blue into a country wedding include blue blossoms in your bouquet, blue ribbons in your hair, blue embroidery on an antique handkerchief, or blue buttercream flowers on your cake.*

Make Your Own Wedding Web Site

A personalized Web site is a good way to keep friends and relatives informed about your wedding plans. You can make it as elaborate and personal as you like, or you can simply post the basic information that guests will need to get to the wedding. Here are some of the topics you might address.

MAPS AND DIRECTIONS. You can type out the directions or include links to Web site that feature maps and driving directions. Depending on the agenda, you may want to include directions to the rehearsal dinner, to weekend activities in the area, to the ceremony, and, if it is in a different location, to the reception as well.

LODGING AND ACCOMMODATIONS. If you have reserved a block of rooms at a particular hotel, include a link for guests to make their reservations. You might also include a link to the local visitors bureau site for any guests who want to find alternative lodging, like a bed and breakfast.

TRAVEL DETAILS. Providing contact information for airlines, trains, or bus lines can be helpful for out-of-town guests. Weather forecasts, too, will let everyone know if they'll need to pack a sweater, an umbrella, or a bathing suit for when they're back at their hotel. Another idea that guests may appreciate: a list of local restaurants.

WEEKEND ITINERARY. If you are planning other events for your guests aside from the wedding, whether it's a farewell brunch the following day or an early-morning round of golf, posting an itinerary can keep guests informed of what's available to them and where they should be at what time.

YOUR LOVE STORY. How did you meet? How did your fiancé propose? Is there special significance to the location of the wedding? Personal anecdotes like these can be fun for guests to read. You might also include an option for guests to post their own memories or well-wishes.

PHOTO GALLERY. Childhood pictures, snapshots from vacations you and your fiancé have taken, a portrait gallery of bridesmaids and groomsmen—all of these can be of interest to your guests. After the wedding, you can post pictures from the celebration and the honeymoon.

OPPOSITE: *White satin ribbons fall from the bride's bouquet, a perfect match for the color of her handmade satin and lace gown. (Trailing ribbons can also be chosen to coordinate with the colors of the flowers a bride will be carrying.) A sheer, floor-length veil adds a touch of drama. At a country wedding, the bride's attire can be as formal or as casual as she wishes.*

～⌒·𝓜usic·⌒～

Music is the soundtrack of your wedding. It sets the mood for the day and signals the transition from ceremony to celebration. Each part of the event should have a distinct musical personality. The solemnity of the ceremony can be reflected in beautiful classical music or favorite romantic songs like Louis Armstrong's "What a Wonderful World." Cocktails should be accompanied by celebratory melodies, upbeat but not too loud so that guests can hear each other speak. Toe-tapping tunes that beckon guests to stand up and dance are characteristic of a great reception. Music can also reflect something personal about the bride and groom. A bride of Irish or Scottish descent, for instance, might choose bagpipes for her processional, while a couple who met in Mexico could hire a mariachi band to enliven the cocktail hour.

Live music is a lovely touch for a country wedding. Even if you choose a deejay for your reception, consider live musicians for your ceremony and cocktail hour. String quartets are a popular choice for ceremonies, and they are also perfectly appropriate for cocktail hour when they can shift tempo and play more contemporary songs. To save money, you might hire a single musician to play a harp, a violin, or—if it is logistically feasible—a piano. Jazz trios are another popular option, especially for cocktail hour.

A great live band at a reception is something guests will never forget. Depending on your taste and the overall theme of your wedding, you might choose a swing band, a salsa band, or a bluegrass band complete with a square-dance caller. When hiring a band, personal recommendations are important. If you (or someone you know) have been to a wedding and loved the band you saw, by all means call the bride or groom to ask for the band's contact information. Don't rely only on a tape of the musicians' music; arrange to see a live performance. Before you make a final decision, be sure your reception site will be able

LEFT: *A wisteria-covered pergola was the perfect setting for a string quartet at this outdoor wedding. When looking for the best place for musicians to sit, choose a spot that is in full view of the festivities but set apart from the foot traffic of waiters and mingling guests.* OPPOSITE: *Under a star-filled sky and paper lanterns in vibrant hues, newlyweds take to the dance floor for their first dance at this vineyard wedding.*

to accommodate the band (if the stage is small, for example, it will limit the number of musicians who can fit there). Also ask in advance about fees, overtime charges, and how food and drinks for the musicians will be handled.

Hiring a deejay tends to cost less than a band, but this option can still create a festive atmosphere for your reception. Nostalgic love songs and favorite dance tunes from the different stages of your life can lead your guests down memory lane as they shimmy the night away. Some couples even create a personal party mix on an MP3 player and hook it up to speakers, in essence becoming their own deejays—the ultimate money-saving tip.

ᴄ Lighting ᴐ

Atmospheric lighting is the finishing touch that showcases all the hard work you've done to create your dream wedding. Thoughtful lighting design is a necessity for evening weddings as well as daytime affairs that will be held indoors or in a tent or barn. Proper illumination may also be required for the safety of your guests; for example, to light pathways at outdoor venues.

Ideally, wedding lighting should cast a soft glow over the festivities. In hotels or other indoor spaces, this means that harsh overhead lights may need to be replaced with pink bulbs or

special spotlights installed by a lighting designer. To find a reputable designer, ask at a local theater company or event planner. Hotels, country clubs, and other indoor venues may have a list of people they've worked with before. Obtain an estimate, speak with references, and ask the designer if he or she has any necessary insurance in place

Paper lanterns. Big or small, all white or rainbow-hued, paper lanterns always add a festive look to any interior or outdoor setting. They can be strung between tent posts or hung from barn rafters or tree branches.

Twinkling lights. Strings of small white holiday lights can be used to great advantage in many places. They can be woven with garlands around tent posts or barn rafters. They can be placed in trees or shrubbery or wound into an archway, under which the couple might take their vows or a cozy seating arrangement might be positioned.

Pinspots. These small spotlights can be used to illuminate each table at the reception (focus on the centerpiece) or other areas you want to draw attention to, such as the wedding cake, the guest book, or the bride and groom's table.

Uplights. When positioned close to the ground, larger spotlights can be used to highlight barn rafters, a room's architectural details, or trees at an outdoor reception. In a tent, colored gels can be placed over uplights to cast a glow of a favorite color (the wedding's theme color, perhaps) onto the ceiling of the tent.

before you make your choice. The following are the main types of lighting that can set a romantic mood.

Candles. Use as many as can safely fit on your dining tables (leaving enough room for wineglasses and other table accessories, of course) to create romantic ambience. Place candles in unexpected spots, such as floating in a pool or pond and suspended in votive holders from the branches of a tree.

ABOVE: *For receptions that will continue past sunset, candlelight casts a romantic glow on the festivities. To shelter candles from evening breezes, place them in votives or hurricane lamps.* OPPOSITE: *Brides and grooms with an eye for design often put their own stamp on some part of their special day, be it custom-designed invitations or a handmade wedding dress. One creative couple even designed the unique lighting that hangs above the tables at their reception.*

Outdoor Survival Guide

An outdoor wedding is a romantic ideal for many people, but a heat wave, an infestation of crawling creatures, or passing showers can sometimes threaten to quite literally rain on your parade. To reduce stress on your big day, our advice is simple: Be prepared for anything.

RAIN. Have alternative sites in mind for both your ceremony and reception. Keep things portable (your ceremony's altar or archway, for instance) in case you need to move them as storm clouds approach. Keep a selection of pretty umbrellas on hand (floral or all-white styles are good choices) if the weather forecast is ominous or if it's a time of year when passing showers are common.

HEAT AND SUN. A few days before your wedding, visit your ceremony site at the same time of day you plan to wed so you can check the angle of the sun. Then determine the placement of your altar and your guest seating to minimize direct sunlight in anyone's eyes. If extreme heat is in the forecast, offer parasols or folding paper fans for chairs that will be in full sun.

COOL TEMPERATURES. A stack of colorful shawls can be a pretty—and practical—detail for an outdoor wedding, especially one that will drift into the evening hours. If you know in advance that the weather may turn cold, consider a tent equipped with heaters.

INSECTS. Before you set a date, find out if there are times of the year when swarming insects can be a problem in the region (along coastal Maine, for example, early June is black fly season). Citronella candles and insect repellent will keep mosquitoes at bay; herbal repellent in attractive bottles tied with pretty ribbon are a nice gesture for your guests.

WIND. In addition to rain or extreme temperatures, consider the possibility of a gusty day. If you wake up to wind on your wedding day, and you're using a tent that has optional side panels, have your tent supplier install them to keep the gusts from blowing through the reception. Consider having a supply of pretty stones on hand to anchor programs to seat cushions and keep place cards from blowing away.

PLEASE TAKE ONE

lavender insect repellent

ABOVE LEFT: *Baskets of parasols stand at the ready for guests at this midsummer ceremony. Doing your best to anticipate heat or chill, rain or shine, is part of planning an outdoor wedding and one that your guests will appreciate.* **ABOVE RIGHT:** *At an outdoor ceremony, prevent programs from blowing away by holding them in place with a polished stone.* **LEFT:** *To ward off insects, have an herbal repellent available for your guests. Look for small bottles or decorative packaging to make the repellent both pretty and practical. Adding citronella candles to tabletop displays can also keep flying pests at bay.*

~ᴄ For Children ᴐ~

Beyond the traditional kids' table, there are many ways to keep children happy, entertained, and nourished at a country wedding. Have a number of fun and unfussy toys on hand—pinwheels, for instance, or sticks with colorful ribbons at one end. An arts and crafts table outfitted with supplies that will keep dress-up clothes clean is another option, like flowers and string to make flower necklaces and head wreaths.

Consider the culinary preferences of the children on your guest list when planning your menu; stock cold bottles of root beer in a tin tub filled with ice and offer a few kid favorites like chicken fingers and French fries. And if you do plan to have a separate kids' table at the dinner hour, decorate it in a festive manner, with garden ornaments like bunnies or gnomes set among the flowers. You can even lay plain paper over the tablecloth and provide jugs filled with crayons.

OPPOSITE: *Pinwheels provide old-fashioned fun to children at outdoor weddings. These pretty vellum examples in shades of blue and purple are gathered in a large canning jar and set atop an antique child's chair.* LEFT: *Flower-shop dog vases from the 1950s and '60s filled with 'Charlotte' roses keep smaller guests company at a kids' table.* ABOVE: *Washtubs filled with icy cold root beer and orange sodas are always a hit with the junior set. Offering special treats to young guests keeps them—and their parents—happy.*

Permits and Insurance

The necessity for permits and insurance will depend largely on where you decide to hold your wedding. Locations that host nuptials on a regular basis (hotels, country clubs, and botanical gardens, for instance) usually take care of such concerns on their own. The further off the beaten path you go, however, the more you will need to look into both of these areas as you plan your special day. Permits may be required to raise a tent in your parents' garden or on a nearby farm; other permits may be needed to accommodate parking or to amplify music. Visit your local town hall to inquire about the specifics regarding party permits. You may be asked about the size of your guest list and the time of day your wedding will take place, so be prepared to answer questions like these.

Insurance for personal injury or for lost or damaged property is worth looking into as well, especially if you plan to hold your wedding in an outdoor setting with rocky or potentially slippery paths. If the wedding will take place at a home or on a farm where there is a house on the property, it may be possible to extend the host's homeowner's insurance policy for the day. Contact your personal insurance agent to learn more or ask friends and family for referrals. Wedding planners and caterers are often familiar with insurance requirements and may know an agent with whom you can consult.

Final Words

No matter how carefully planned an event may be, unexpected issues can sometimes crop up at the last minute to threaten the tranquility of the day. It might be rain clouds on the horizon, a torn seam in a wedding gown, or a delivery person calling to say he or she is lost. You may have seen an example of this when you were a guest or an attendant at someone else's wedding. If that is the case, you probably know that in the end, everything generally works out just fine. The same will be true at your wedding. If anything out of the ordinary happens, remember that the day is about more than hosting a great party, it is about you and your fiancé joining together to meet the challenges of life—both great and small. Take a deep breath, laugh if you can, and ask guests and attendants for help if there is a problem to be solved.

OPPOSITE: *When planning an outdoor ceremony, visit the location at different times of the day to determine which appeals to you the most. This couple chose late afternoon for their beach wedding to coincide with the sun setting in the west and the moon rising in the east. Beach grass is interwoven among the bridal bouquet's white calla lilies, roses, and orchids, adding personal significance to the arrangement.*

Photography Credits

Page 78 (clockwise from top left): Steven Randazzo; Charles Maraia; Steven Randazzo

Page 79: Gertrude & Mabel Photography

Page 81: Jim Bastardo

Page 82: Natasha Milne (left); Charles Maraia (right)

Page 83: Debra McClinton

Page 85: Gertrude & Mabel Photography

Page 86 (clockwise from top left): Jim Bastardo; Gertrude & Mabel Photography; Natasha Milne

Page 87: Gertrude & Mabel Photography

Page 88: Gertrude & Mabel Photography

Page 89: Orchard Cove Photography

Page 90: Debra McClinton

Page 91 (clockwise from top left): Ryan Benyi; Orchard Cove Photography; John Dolan

Page 92: Charles Maraia

Page 93: Laura Moss

Page 95: Charles Maraia

Page 96: Tec Petaja

Page 99: Natasha Milne (left); Jim Bastardo (right):

Page 102: Lisa Lefkowitz (left); Gertrude & Mabel Photography (right)

Page 103 (from top): Debra McClinton; Gertrude & Mabel Photography Photography

Page 104: Jim Bastardo

Page 105: Debra McClinton

Page 105: Aimée Herring

Page 106: Laura Moss

Page 107: Gertrude & Mabel Photography

Page 109: John Granen (2)

Page 110: Jim Bastardo

Page 111: Natasha Milne (2)

Page 112 (clockwise from top left): Gertrude & Mabel Photography ; Laura Moss; Gertrude & Mabel Photography

Page 114: Helen Norman

Page 115: Ryan Benyi

Page 116: Gertrude & Mabel Photography

Page 120: Jim Bastardo

Page 123 Debra McClinton

Page 124: Debra McClinton

Page 125 (from top): Helen Norman; Debra McClinton

Page 127: Jim Bastardo

Page 128: Ryan Benyi

Page 129: John Granen

Page 130: John Granen

Page 131: Gertrude & Mabel Photography

Page 133: Tec Petaja (3)

Page 134: Debra McClinton

Page 135: Charles Maraia (left); Laura Moss (right)

Page 136: Carleen Childs

Page 144: Gertrude & Mabel Photography

Index

Design by Sara Gillingham.

Library of Congress Cataloging-in-Publication Data
Proeller Hueston, Marie.
   Weddings : ideas & inspirations for celebrating in style / Marie Proeller
Hueston.
   p. cm. -- (Country living)
   Includes index.
   ISBN 978-1-58816-745-3
   1. Weddings--Planning. I. Title.
   HQ745.P76 2010
   395.2'2--dc22
2009019546

10 9 8 7 6 5 4 3 2 1

Published by Hearst Books
A division of Sterling Publishing Co., Inc.
387 Park Avenue South, New York, NY 10016

Country Living is a registered trademark of Hearst Communications, Inc.

www.countryliving.com

For information about custom editions, special sales, premium and corporate
purchases, please contact Sterling Special Sales Department at 800-805-5489 or
specialsales@sterlingpub.com.

Distributed in Canada by Sterling Publishing
^{c}/o Canadian Manda Group, 165 Dufferin Street
Toronto, Ontario, Canada M6K 3H6

Distributed in Australia by Capricorn Link (Australia) Pty. Ltd.
P.O. Box 704, Windsor, NSW 2756 Australia

Manufactured in China

Sterling ISBN 978-1-58816-745-3